THE UNLIMITED POWER OF THE BLOOD

Colin Dye

Dovewell Publications

Dovewell Publications
PO Box 9161
London
W3 6GS
England

Scriptural quotations are from the New King James Version, Thomas Nelson Inc., 1991.

ISBN 1 898 444 90 0

Produced and printed by Gazelle Creative Productions Ltd, Concorde House, Grenville Place, Mill Hill, London, NW7 3SA

CONTENTS

1

The blood and the cross

There cannot be many people in the world who do not recognise that a simple wooden cross is the universal symbol of the Christian faith. And there surely cannot be even a single believer who has never heard about the precious blood of Jesus.

You'll already know, my friend, that Jesus shed His blood on the cross for your complete-and-eternal salvation. But do you know the *full* power of His blood? And have you fully entered into the blessings which have come to you by the blood?

I'm sure that you've already experienced many special blessings, but God has planned for you to receive every *good thing* – and He has purchased these blessings for you with the blood which was shed on the cross. This means, dear friend, that you owe *everything* to the blood and to the cross!

An amazing discovery

Right at this moment, you're holding in your hands a quite amazing discovery. As you turn the pages and read the chapters of this book, you'll begin to glimpse the *unlimited* power of the blood.

When you finally grasp that the blood of Jesus really has *no limits*, you'll never again allow yourself to be limited in your faith! Praise God!

In this book, I'm going to reveal some astonishing biblical revelations about 'the blood and the cross'. As you receive and apply these special truths:

⇒ *you'll experience new boldness in faith*

⇒ *you'll have complete assurance in prayer*

⇒ *you'll deal with all your negative thoughts*

⇒ *you'll become positive, healthy and confident*

⇒ *you'll know that you're completely accepted by God*

By the end of this book, my dear friend, you'll have tipped your doubts into a dustbin, and you'll have begun to grasp the extraordinary greatness of your eternal salvation.

You'll have absolute, 100% assurance that God loves you. You'll be completely certain that He's made full provision for *every* area of your life. And you'll know that Christ's precious blood is the binding guarantee that *all* the promises of God's Word are for *you* – and that they *will* be fulfilled in your life!

The blood

Many believers use phrases like 'washed in the blood', 'covered by the blood' and 'pleading the blood'. These lovely words express important truths, but they can confuse and mislead those people who don't know what they mean.

When we speak about 'the blood', we're referring to the blood which poured from Jesus' wounds when He was nailed to the cross of Calvary. But most of us don't have only this literal meaning in mind when we speak about 'the blood'.

Instead, we normally use 'the blood' as a short-hand expression for the *complete sacrificial death of Jesus*. For us, the phrase 'the blood' represents the totality of Christ's death on the cross: quite simply, the two little words 'the blood' represent *everything* that God endured and achieved for us through the cross.

A crimson thread

Some believers think about the blood and the cross only in terms of the New Testament. But an unbroken crimson thread runs through the whole Bible, and the shadow of the cross falls upon every page.

In this book, I'm going to show you how the story of the blood and the cross develops. You'll learn about God's gracious blood-stained hands in the garden of Eden. You'll see the blood on Mount Ararat as Noah rejoices at his deliverance in a time of judgement. And you'll read about holy fire passing between broken pieces of animals as God covenants with Abraham.

Then, on the very mountain where the cross will be raised two thousand years later, you'll see the shadow of the cross in the binding of Isaac and in the death of the God-provided substitute ram.

You'll notice the crimson thread again in Egypt, when the blood on Israel's homes turns away the angel of death; and then in Sinai when the people of God sprinkle themselves to acknowledge their debt of obedience at the giving of the Law.

You'll discover that the joyous worship of God – from Leviticus to Malachi – is completely drenched with blood. And you'll recognise how these important Old Testament stories prepare us for the shedding of Christ's perfect blood on the cross.

Then I'll show you that 'the blood of the cross' is the focus of everything Jesus came to do, and that it is the common theme of all the apostles. You'll also notice that the book of Hebrews contains many whole chapters about the blood, and that the book of Revelation centres on the Lamb who was slain.

When you've finished reading this book, dear friend, you'll be fully convinced that 'the blood' is one of the central themes of the Word of God!

Life-giving blood

Before we start, however, you need to understand why the biblical stories about the blood are so important and significant.

First, all the Old Testament *sacrifices* and *covenants* are 'pictures' of the cross, of the place where Jesus shed his blood as the full-and-final sacrifice and as the new covenant. This means that everything the Old Testament records about the blood reveals something important about the cross.

Second, blood represents and contains *life*: it's the difference between life and death. If you were badly injured in an accident, and your blood drained away, you would die. Similarly, if doctors had to operate on you, they might need to give you a transfusion of another person's blood to keep you alive.

The life of the flesh is in the blood   Leviticus 17:11

This explains why the Bible places such a high value on blood. It teaches that the blood of a human is more valuable than that of an animal, and that the blood of God's only Son is the most precious life-giving commodity of all.

Finally, God has declared that blood is the price and the means of *atonement*. This old word refers to the process by which God and humanity become 'fully united' or 'completely one'.

The life of the flesh is in the blood, and I have given it to you upon the altar to make atonement for your souls; for it is the blood that makes atonement for the soul.   Leviticus 17:11

Quite simply, God has ordained that sacrifice, that the shedding of blood, is the only way by which sinful men and women can be made one with Him.

Praise God, my friend, for you know what's happened. You already know the deep truths that:

⇒ *in Christ, God Himself provided the blood of the sacrifice so that you could be one with Him for ever*

⇒ *on the cross, Christ willingly donated every drop of His blood so that you could always have His life flowing through you*

These wonderful truths ensure that our thinking about the blood in this book will not be a morbid exercise; instead, it will be a time of praise and rejoicing!

When we consider the blood, we'll be considering what God has done for you in salvation – and praise and thanksgiving are the only right human responses.

So, my dear friend, settle down in your chair; make yourself comfortable; and prepare yourself for the blood's unlimited power.

2

The blood and unlimited blessing

When you think about the Jewish blood sacrifices, do they suggest death and destruction to you? Do you imagine that people offered these sacrifices just to earn God's forgiveness and favour?

If this were true, what would it say about the cross? That it was a place of hopeless death and decay? And that Christ was trying to persuade a reluctant God to forgive humanity?

No! Sacrificial blood speaks of *life* because it brings life; and the Old Testament blood sacrifices were *God's* personal blessing to His people.

The first sacrifice

Sacrifice began with God, my friend, not with men and women, for it was God who shed the first blood, God who made the first sacrifice, God who endured the first grief of loss. And He did these things to bless a pair of sinners with lasting hope.

Can you imagine what it must have been like in Eden? The garden was perfect: there was no evil, no wickedness, no deceit, no sickness, no sin. The first humans were completely pure, and they lived in a wonderful, intimate relationship with God.

One day, however, Adam and Eve succumbed to the devil's temptations and disobeyed God. They sinned – and tasted sin's bitter consequences of shame, guilt and fear. In despair, they covered themselves with leaves and tried to hide from God.

In His justice, God cursed humanity and expelled the pair from Eden. But, in His grace, He offered them tunics as a covering for sin and a uniform for a new task – the fruit of the first blood sacrifice.

For Adam and his wife, the Lord God made tunics of skin and clothed them.　　　　Genesis 3:21

Some perfect animals must have died to provide this covering of grace. And it must have been God who slew, then skinned, the precious, perfect creatures that He'd only just made and blessed.

This gift of blood-stained clothes is our first sighting of the crimson thread which leads to Calvary, our first insight into men and women being covered by the blood and clothed for service.

Can you see, dear friend, how this blessing establishes the pattern of the blood and the cross?

⇒ *those who benefited from the blood were completely undeserving – so are you!*

⇒ *those who suffered were perfect and blameless – so is He!*

⇒ *the price was high, for both the giver and the gift – and at Calvary!*

⇒ *grace, love and mercy motivated the sacrifice – so too the cross!*

⇒ *the pair had the freedom to accept or reject the fruit of the blood – and so have you!*

⇒ *the gift not only dealt with their sin, it also equipped them to serve God in a new way – it's the same for you!*

Promises of blessing

According to the Bible, Cain and Abel both presented gifts to God, but God looked favourably only on Abel's sacrifice.

Have you ever wondered why God preferred Abel's gift? It was because Cain gave God only some produce of the soil, whereas Abel sacrificed the valuable *first-born* of his flock.

By faith Abel offered to God a more excellent sacrifice than Cain, through which he obtained witness that he was righteous.   Hebrews 11:4

God didn't need what Cain and Abel were offering Him in thanksgiving; but He deserved the best, and Abel's was the more valuable gift.

God was so delighted with Abel's faith-filled blood sacrifice, that He declared him *righteous*. Whenever we notice the crimson thread in the Scriptures, we see God rewarding human faith with similar *promises of righteousness and blessing*.

It was the same for Noah. After the flood had subsided, he offered God a sacrifice in thanks for his safe deliverance. God was so pleased with Noah's obedient sacrifice that He rewarded him and his sons with the promise of blessing.

God blessed Noah and his sons, and said to them: "Be fruitful and multiply, and fill the earth".
                                            Genesis 9:1

Can you guess, my friend, how God will respond to Christ's sacrifice on the cross? Will it be with a tight-lipped smile? Or with extravagant promises of blessing for *all* who are joined to Him by faith?

Unlimited blessing

Abraham must have been in the habit of offering God sacrifices of praise, or Isaac would not have asked his father why they'd not brought a lamb.

They'd no animal because God had ordered Abraham to sacrifice Isaac on Mount Moriah – the area where the Jerusalem Temple would be built.

Isaac, who by then was about thirty, was prepared to be bound on the altar as the willing victim. And the father was ready to sacrifice his beloved Son.

They did not understand why this was happening, but they believed that God knew best. So, *by faith*, Abraham seized the knife, raised it high, and prepared to plunge it into his son.

Wonderfully, God's grace intervened. God provided a substitute ram for the sacrifice, and then rewarded Abraham with *unlimited blessing*.

Abraham and Isaac had been ready for death without any reward – loving obedience was their only motivation. But God responded to faith-filled obedience with an amazing prom...

In blessing I will bless you, and in multiplying I will multiply your descendants... In your seed all the nations of the earth shall be blessed because you have obeyed My voice.   Genesis 22:17-18

What a picture of the cross! If God poured such blessing on Abraham and Isaac's willingness to obey Him (blessing which overflowed to their descendants), can you imagine the blessings which will flow to Jesus and to His seed because of His willing obedience on the very same mountain?

Abraham called the place 'The Lord will provide'... In the Mount of the Lord it shall be provided.   Genesis 22:14

Pointers to the cross

You're only half-way through Genesis, my friend, and you've already seen that the Old Testament blood sacrifices point straight to the cross.

After just a few pages of this book, you've grasped that the blood of the cross means unlimited grace and unlimited blessing. This must be a very good reason for offering God unlimited praise!

3

The blood and unlimited salvation

I'm sure you know that, early in their history, the people of Israel were slaves in Egypt. Eventually, God revealed Himself to Moses and appointed him to lead the people away from slavery and into the promised land of Canaan.

Moses spoke to Pharaoh, the Egyptian ruler, but he would not let the people of Israel go. So God sent a series of warning 'plagues' to Egypt.

When Pharaoh still refused to release the Israelites, God announced that He would send a final 'plague' of death on the country. There would be a supreme act of holy judgement on

Egypt *and* a merciful act of deliverance for Israel. God would act decisively to demonstrate His love *and* His justice, His grace *and* His holiness.

God told Moses that each Israelite household should take a perfect lamb or goat, kill it, and sprinkle some of its blood on the outside doorposts and lintels of their hoses.

Sprinkled with the blood

That night, God passed through Egypt and killed the firstborn male of every human family and every farm animal. But He passed over *all* those homes where the doorways were splashed with blood.

There was *unlimited salvation* from death, my friend, for all the households whose homes were sprinkled with the blood of a lamb! Hallelujah!

Just as Adam and Eve in Eden had personally to accept the blood-stained clothes from God, so each Jewish family had personally to act on God's provision of the blood sacrifice.

They each had to sacrifice their most valuable animal and sprinkle its blood on their doorposts: this was their personal, faith-filled response to God's outstretched grace.

And, again, the Bible records that God rewarded His people's obedient sacrifices with unlimited blessing – this time with a personal salvation from death *and* a corporate salvation from slavery.

Pointers to the cross

Isn't this another amazing picture of the cross and our unlimited salvation!

⇒ *there was only one way of escape from God's just wrath, that was by God's gracious provision – it's still the same today!*

⇒ *God's merciful love passed over every blood-marked home to shield them from His wrath – it's still the same today!*

⇒ *the people of Israel belonged to God because they'd been purchased by the blood and so were consecrated to His service – it's still the same today!*

⇒ *the only survivors were those in homes where a perfect lamb had died instead of them – it's still the same today!*

⇒ *the survivors were those who'd appropriated the blood – it's still the same today!*

⇒ *the sacrifice not only dealt with their past bondage, it also provided them with a new life of freedom – yes, it's still the same today!*

My dear friend, the judgement of God and the sentence of death hangs over every household today. There isn't a person alive on earth who doesn't live in the fear and knowledge of death.

The wonderful news, however, is that the perfect Lamb has been sacrificed at Calvary; and that all those who believe His blood was shed to achieve their unlimited salvation will be spared when the terrible day of judgement finally comes.

Claim the blood

Make sure that you claim His blood, my friend, and that you claim it for your entire household. Do it now before you read another page.

Sprinkle the blood of the Lamb over your life and over your home. Place it over yourself and your loved ones. Live continually in the safety of its covering. And make sure that you spread the good news of His saving blood to all your friends and relations.

Once you've started to believe in the blood, and have personally appropriated it, you'll begin to sleep easy at night. You'll rest in the knowledge that His blood is the guarantee of your unlimited salvation and your unlimited new life of freedom.

4

The blood and unlimited worship

After God had saved the Israelites from slavery and death by the blood of the Passover lambs, they spent many years wandering in the wilderness.

During this time, God gave Moses clear instructions about the offering of sacrifices. He laid down that four special offerings should be made which involved the shedding of blood.

⇒ *the holocaust, or burnt offering*

⇒ *the communion, or peace offering*

⇒ *the sin offering*

⇒ *the guilt, reparation or trespass offering*

God declared that these sacrifices should be offered personally and nationally, privately and publicly, regularly and as special needs arose. There were to be weekly, monthly and annual public sacrifices. And the Passover was to be celebrated privately within the family home.

God gave His people these sacrifices to use when they needed to seal their promises and release themselves from vows; when they wanted to express praise, thanksgiving and repentance; when they needed to dedicate their children, priests, kings, and so on. Whatever the reason, whenever the people turned to God, they worshipped Him with the sacrifices that He'd given them to use.

The ritual of worship

When one of God's people was moved to worship Him, they selected the most valuable animal from their flocks and brought it to the designated place.

Then they laid their hands on the animal to show that it was their representative or *substitute*. If they were making a sin or guilt offering, they confessed their sins symbolically to transfer the legal consequences of their sins to the animal.

Next, they personally killed the animal. The priests collected the shed blood in a basin and splashed it against the opposite corners of the altar so that all four sides were sprinkled with blood.

The priests then burnt the fat; if it was a holocaust offering, they burnt everything. Finally, the priests ate the meat; if it was a communion offering, the priests and the worshipper ate the meat together.

Special purposes

Each of the four blood sacrifices had a special use and purpose for the people of God.

God gave them the *holocaust* to use in praise and thanksgiving: it represented the dedication by the worshipper, and the acceptance by God, of everything that they had and were. The whole of this offering ascended to God as a pleasing aroma – it was *all for Him*!

God gave them the *communion* to use in consecration and cleansing: the eating together by priests and people reminded the worshipper to live in close communion with God and other people.

The *sin* and *guilt* offerings, however, had a far deeper purpose, for God gave these to His people to cover their sins and make restitution for their guilt. These offerings enabled worshippers to display their sense of separation from God (a separation caused by their sin), and to cry for it to be covered.

A temporary covering of grace

It's important you grasp that the blood of the sacrifices was *God's gracious provision* to cover His people's sin and make restitution for their guilt.

Don't ever think that the people of Israel made blood sacrifices to try and persuade God to do something that He didn't want to do! No, when they made these sacrifices they were merely obeying God's instructions and eagerly seizing the blessings that He had provided for them.

Just as the first sacrifice was offered by God's blood-stained hands as a makeshift cover for Adam's sinful condition, so – through the blood sacrifices – God provided His people with another means of temporarily covering their sin and shame.

But, my dear friend, please recognise that none of these offerings, no matter how correctly and sincerely they were offered, could permanently take away the people's sin or fully achieve their appointed purpose.

The blood sacrifices were merely a temporary measure which awaited the One whose offering on a cross would *permanently* deal with sin and guilt, and would *eternally* open the door to unlimited worship in the very presence of God. Hallelujah!

Shouldn't you thank God, my friend, that you live in these days, when the shed blood of Christ permanently guarantees your eternal forgiveness, eternally removes your guilt, and beckons you into the welcoming presence of God to dwell with Him, face-to-face, forever!

5

The blood and unlimited sin bearing

We all have special days which we anticipate with great excitement – annual epics like our birthday and Christmas, and once-in-a-lifetime events like marriage and retirement.

By far the most important event for the people of Israel was their annual 'Day of Atonement' – there was nothing quite like it!

This was a once-a-year *national* sacrifice for sin (in contrast to the regular *personal* sacrifices), and was the only occasion when the 'holy of holies' was entered – and then only by the high priest.

The centre-piece of the ceremony was the moment when the high priest sacrificed two goats to cover *all* the sins of the *whole* people of Israel, and then passed through the veil and entered into the holy of holies.

First, the high priest slaughtered one goat and sprinkled its blood on the altar. Then he placed his hands on the other goat, confessed all the wickedness and rebellion of God's people, and drove the goat into the desert so that it would symbolically bear all their sins away.

Although two goats were sacrificed, it was a single sacrifice for sin which both *covered* the sin and *bore it away*. As a result, the high priest could enter into the holy presence of God to demonstrate the reconciliation of God and His people.

Another pointer to the cross

Isn't this another amazing picture of the cross! The details are buried deep in the book of Leviticus, and I doubt whether many believers dig there that often for treasure.

But you should try, my friend, for the shadow of the cross is plainly seen throughout Leviticus – especially in chapter 16!

The great-and-abiding revelation of the Day of Atonement is that reconciliation with God is possible only through the single sacrifice of a substitute which involves the bearing of sin.

It reveals for all time that the atoning process, so graciously provided by God, involves a substitute:

⇒ *confession of sin by the high priest*

⇒ *carrying away of the burden of sin by one creature*

⇒ *bearing of the punishment of sin by another creature*

I'm sure you've already realised that this epic once-a-year adventure points straight to the once-and-for-all blood sacrifice of Jesus on the cross.

He's the high priest, dear friend, who's made the fullest possible confession of all your sin!

He's the One who's carried *all* your sins away, so that they can be seen and remembered no more.

He's the Substitute who's willingly endured the just punishment which is due to all your sin.

And He's the high priest who's gone through the veil so that *you* can follow Him into the presence of God – certain of forgiveness and acceptance.

Praise His wonderful name!

The sin-bearing Servant

Although the Day of Atonement was a very special day, and was God's gracious provision for dealing with the whole nation's sin, it must have been clear to many Jews that a goat was a rather poor substitute for a human.

After several generations, God sent the prophet Isaiah to prepare Israel for a human servant who would suffer, bear sin and die for men and women.

This servant's suffering and death are described in Isaiah chapter 53. No other Old Testament passage points more clearly to the cross and reveals the crimson thread so plainly.

No chapter is mentioned more frequently in the New Testament; so turn to your Bible now, dear friend, and read Isaiah 53 several times.

This great prophecy of the blood and the cross reveals that the Suffering Servant of God will:

⇒ *bear your griefs*

⇒ *carry your sorrows*

⇒ *be wounded for your transgressions*

⇒ *be bruised for your iniquities*

⇒ *be bruised for your iniquities*

⇒ *be chastised for your peace*

⇒ *be whipped for your healing*

⇒ *carry your iniquities*

⇒ *be stricken for your transgressions*

⇒ *bear your iniquities*

⇒ *bear your sin*

I'm sure you know that Jesus is this Suffering Servant! On the cross, He died in your place, on your behalf, as your perfect substitute. He bore the full penalty due to your rebellion and sin and the full weight of the pain of your sin.

Why has He done this for you, my friend? Why has He given every drop of His blood to save your life? The answer is simple: it's because He loves you with an everlasting passion: He thinks that you're special, and that you're worth all the pain He's endured.

Isn't He wonderful! Doesn't He deserve your full devotion and your unceasing praise?

6

The sacrificial blood of God-in-Christ

Every appearance of the crimson thread in the Old Testament prepares the way for the New Testament declaration that Jesus Christ shed His blood as a sacrifice for you – and for all people everywhere.

All the Jewish sacrifices are meant to point you to Christ: they should help you grasp the significance of His death, and understand why He died.

What they don't do, however, is reveal precisely who Jesus is. Most unbelievers think that He was merely a man; while many believers imagine that He was somehow independent of God.

Right and wrong ideas

The problem with these ideas, my dear friend, is that they lead people to misunderstand the blood.

Never think that, on the cross, Jesus was trying to pacify an angry God and grasp a begrudging salvation. And never think that an unjust God killed an innocent Jesus in place of the real culprits.

Remember, the story of Abraham and Isaac on Mount Moriah paved the way for the truth. The Father was ready to sacrifice His beloved Son *and* the adult Son was prepared to be the willing victim.

Their wills were one: the Father gave the Son *and* the Son freely gave Himself. The Father sacrificed the Son and the Son willingly sacrificed Himself.

God was in Christ reconciling the world to Himself, not imputing their trespasses to them.
2 Corinthians 5:19

This should help you to realise that the blood sacrifice on the cross was not made by Christ alone or by God alone, but by God acting in Christ.

In their love for you, my friend, the Father, the Son and the Spirit worked *together* in grace and harmony in the shedding of their own blood.

33

God in Christ

Some people have suggested that God died on the cross, but common sense should convince you that the immortal God could not die.

God simply had to become fully human (without ceasing to be fully God) if He was to die as your substitute atoning sacrifice, and be both Judge *and* innocent victim, both high priest *and* perfect lamb.

Jesus Christ, being in the form of God, did not consider it robbery to be equal with God, but made Himself of no reputation, taking the form of a servant, and coming in the likeness of men. And being found in appearance as a man, He humbled Himself and became obedient to the point of death, even the death of the cross. Philippians 2:6-8

When you think about it carefully, my friend, it should be obvious that only a human *should* atone for your sins (because it's you who's sinned). And that only God *could* accomplish the necessary atonement (since it's He who's justly demanded it).

God-in-Christ, therefore, is the only substitute who can accomplish your atonement, because Jesus is the only One in whom the *should* and the *could* are united by His fully-human, fully-divine nature.

Your substitute on the cross

The good news, dear friend, is that a substitute has taken your place, offered your confession, borne the pain of your sin, and endured the penalty due to your disobedience. And this substitute wasn't an animal, nor was it Christ alone or God alone.

Instead, the substitute who died in your place was *God-in-Christ* – the fully-human, fully-divine being who was uniquely qualified to represent human you and divine God, and to mediate between you.

When God gave His Son for you, dear friend, He graciously gave Himself! When He sent His Son for you, He graciously came Himself! God humbled Himself to become – in-and-through His Son – human flesh, and to endure and accept the terrible consequences of all your sin.

In His amazing grace, the Judge personally intervened and endured the penalty which He'd imposed upon you. In order to save you from death, my friend, God-in-Christ graciously substituted Himself and shed His blood for you.

How can you respond to the cross and the blood with anything other than total commitment?

Your faith declaration

"I confess and declare that I owe everything to the precious blood of Jesus Christ, who died in my place, once-and-for-all, on the cross of Calvary.

I thank You, my Father, for graciously providing the blood of sacrifice so that I can dwell in Your presence forever.

I thank You, my Jesus, for willingly donating every drop of Your blood so that I can always have Your life flowing through me.

I thank You, my God, for providing the Passover Lamb to die for my life and my deliverance. I sprinkle His blood over my life, over my home, over my family, over all that is dear to me. I receive by faith the unlimited salvation and unlimited blessings that His shed blood brings to me.

I affirm before all the host of heaven that the precious blood of Jesus permanently guarantees my forgiveness, eternally removes my guilt, and beckons me into the welcoming presence of God.

In Your grace and mercy, through the great power of the blood, You have provided me with unlimited life and freedom. I accept Your gift. I receive Your gift. I depend on Your gift. I rejoice in Your gift. Praise Your wonderful name."

7

The blood and the covenant

By now, my friend, you should have grasped that the Old Testament blood sacrifices prepare the way for Christ's sacrificial death on the cross. They express a need which only He fully satisfies, embody a faith which He alone can justify, and demand a lifestyle which only He makes possible.

You can see the crimson thread, however, not only in the Old Testament *sacrifices*, but also in the Old Testament *covenants*.

During the 'Last Supper', when Jesus and His apostles had gathered together to eat the Passover meal, Jesus took a loaf of bread, gave thanks for it, broke it into pieces, and handed it round, saying:

Take, eat; this is My body which is broken for you; do this in remembrance of Me. 1 Corinthians 11:24

In the same way, after the Passover meal, Jesus took a cup of wine, gave thanks for it, passed it to His apostles, and said:

This is My blood of the new covenant, which is shed for many for the remission of sins.

Matthew 26:28

Holy communion

Whenever you celebrate communion, dear friend, you're meant to remember Christ's broken body which – like the Passover lambs – accomplished your deliverance from slavery and death.

But, more than this, you're meant to rejoice in the blood through which God established a *new covenant* with you which promises forgiveness.

Because Christ has commanded us to remember His death (especially His broken body and His shed blood), our times of communion together should be exuberant, passionate, joyous celebrations which publicly celebrate all the great achievements of His precious blood! Let's make them more like this!

Binding agreements

The apostles knew what Jesus meant when He told them that God was making a 'new covenant' with them through the shedding of His blood in death.

They knew that a covenant was *a binding agreement* and they were familiar with the other covenants that God had made with His people.

Today, however, many people are not that familiar with the Old Testament, so we need to consider the 'old covenants' to appreciate how they reveal the crimson thread and pave the way for the cross.

The first covenant

God made His first covenant with Noah, just before the flood, and it came like a bolt from the blue.

I Myself am bringing the flood of waters on the earth... and everything that is on earth shall die. But I will establish My covenant with you; and you shall go into the ark – you, your sons, your wife, and your sons' wives with you.   Genesis 6:17-18

God simply announced to Noah that He was making a binding agreement with him. It was God's covenant, He established it entirely on His own. And the covenant was *God's binding promise* to keep Noah's family safe in a time of judgement.

Even though the covenant was 'all-grace', Noah's family had to respond by entering the ark to experience the benefits of *covenant salvation*.

Just as the Jews in Egypt had to sprinkle the blood on their homes to be kept safe in the day of judgement, so Noah's family had to appropriate God's promise of safety by faith-filled obedience.

Do you see the principle, dear friend? Can you see that it's still the same for you? Through the blood, God has made provision for your full-and-eternal salvation – but (like Noah and the Jews) you still have to appropriate His gift by faith, and still have to enter into the new life that He offers.

The covenant repeated

After the Flood had subsided, God repeated His covenant promise to Noah and his family.

Behold, I establish My covenant with you and with your descendants after you.   Genesis 9:9

The first half of Genesis chapter nine describes this 'old covenant', and reports that God provided *a visible sign* of the promise.

Read the passage now, dear friend, and see how it prepares the way for the 'new covenant' in the blood for the remission of sins. Notice how God's binding agreement with Noah is:

⇒ *willed, initiated and established entirely by God Himself – it's the same with the new covenant that God's made with you!*

⇒ *universal in scope; it embraces not only Noah but also his family and descendants – it's the same for you; remember, God's promised you 'household salvation'!*

⇒ *unconditional; there are no pre-conditions or requirements – it's still the same for you!*

⇒ *accompanied by a confirming sign; the rainbow could not be controlled by humanity, and was God's guarantee of His faithfulness – God has given you, my friend, an even greater sign of His faithfulness, for He's given you the Holy Spirit!*

⇒ *everlasting – it's still the same for you, the new covenant is for ever and cannot be broken! Hallelujah!*

8

The blood covenant

God spoke to Abraham while he was living with his parents in Haran (he was still called Abram then).

Get out of your country, from your kindred and your father's house, to a land that I will show you. I will make you a great nation; I will bless you and make your name great... in you all the families of the earth shall be blessed. Genesis 12:1-3

Abram responded to God's Word with faith-filled obedience, and left Haran for Canaan. Many years later, God confirmed His promise to Abram; but this time Abram questioned God about the way that He would fulfil the promise.

God took Abram outside and told him to look at the night sky. Through seeing the stars, Abram 'saw' God's promise to him, and he believed that it would be fulfilled.

The Bible comments that Abram put his faith in God at this moment, and that this was credited to him as righteousness.

Despite his faith, Abram still asked God for some sort of guarantee of assurance. He wanted a sign which would confirm God's Word.

In reality, my friend, Abram was asking God to enter into a binding agreement with him. Abram wanted to be certain that God's promise would be fulfilled.

Sacrifice and covenant

The Bible reports that God responded to Abram's request with a covenant, and this is described in the second half of Genesis chapter fifteen. Read this now, and see how sacrificial blood is involved in God's covenant activity.

The covenant ceremony was similar to a ritual which was often used in those days. When two people wanted to make a binding agreement, they both passed between the parts of a slaughtered animal and called down the fate of the sacrificial victim on themselves if they broke the agreement.

In His ceremony with Abram, however, only God passed between the animal parts to show that His covenant was a unilateral action. It was all God; it was all-grace.

I'm sure you spotted the shadow of the cross in this story, and recognised that the flame was *Yahweh* Himself. But did you notice that the darkness and length of time also pointed to Calvary? That was the moment when God made a similar all-grace covenant with *you* through the shed blood and broken body of Jesus. Hallelujah!

The blood is the sign

In His covenant with Abram, dear friend, it was as though God was saying, 'Let me be as these broken pieces of animals if I fail to fulfil My Word to you.'

In this way, the blood covenant anticipated God's solemn oath at the completion of Abram's faith.

By Myself I have sworn, because you have done this thing, and have not withheld your son... in blessing I will bless you, and in multiplying I will multiply your descendants as the stars of the heaven...   Genesis 22:16-17

The story of this old covenant should help you to realise that Christ's blood is God's solemn pledge to you that He will keep His new covenant promise of forgiveness.

When you see the blood, you see the guarantee of your forgiveness! When you're covered with the blood, you're covered with God's binding agreement to forgive you!

Always remember, my friend, that *the blood is a God-given aid to your faith.*

Even though you've responded to God with faith and have been declared righteous, I'm sure there are times when you still need some sort of re-assurance that you really have been forgiven.

Look at the blood, dear friend, look at the blood! It's the eternal guarantee of your permanent, unconditional forgiveness. Hallelujah!

You should also be able to see from Abram's story that the blood of the covenant is not only a guarantee of forgiveness. As well as this, it also anticipates God's 'oath', his 'rainbow' in your life, the fullness of the Spirit in your life!

9

The old covenant

I'm sure you've heard about 'the old covenant', and know that it refers to the binding agreement which God made with His people Israel.

Many people think that the old covenant was entirely different from God's new covenant with you and me. They think that God acted in one way then, and in a completely different way in Christ.

If this were true, however, it would mean that the covenant with Israel didn't relate to the covenants with Noah and Abram, didn't pave the way for the new covenant, and didn't point to the blood and the cross. In fact, it would mean that the old covenant was the spiritual equivalent of a blind alley!

The Old Testament, however, plainly shows that all God's dealings with Israel were based on the promise which was contained in His unconditional, all-grace, blood covenant with Abram.

I appeared to Abraham... I have also established My covenant with them, to give them the land of Canaan... And I have also heard the groaning of the children of Israel... and I have remembered My covenant. Therefore say to the children of Israel: "I am the Lord; I will bring you out... I will rescue you... I will redeem you... I will take you as My people... I will bring you into the land which I swore to give to Abraham..." Exodus 6:3-8

This should convince you that God's covenant with the children of Abraham, through Moses, continued, developed and adjusted the binding agreement that He'd previously made with their forefather Abraham.

Several stages

You've already seen, my friend, that God made one covenant with Noah in two stages before and after the flood; and that He made one covenant with Abraham, which He later bound Himself to in blood, and then, later still, affirmed with an oath.

In a similar way, God made one covenant with Israel in several stages. The details of these different stages may vary but the principles of *grace* and *great blessing* run through them all.

Ask yourself, dear friend, what this process suggests to you about the new covenant.

⇒ *Does it point to one huge blessing, which was given to you in a flash at conversion?*

⇒ *Or does it point to your wonderful new birth by the Spirit and also to your filling with the Holy Spirit?*

God repeated and developed His covenant promises to Israel through Moses over many years. First, we see that God guaranteed:

You shall be a special treasure to Me above all people; for all the earth is Mine. And you shall be to Me a kingdom of priests and a holy nation.
Exodus 19:5-6

Next we see that the old covenant was sealed in sacrificial blood.

Moses took the blood, sprinkled it on the people, and said, "Behold, the blood of the covenant which the Lord has made with you". Exodus 24:8

48

Then, many years later, we see that God said:

Behold I make a covenant. Before all your people I will do marvels such as have not been done in all the earth... all the people among whom you are shall see the work of the Lord... It is an awesome thing that I will do with you.   Exodus 34:10

You should be gasping with wonder at these promises dear friend – especially when you realise that God bound Himself to them in blood – for they point straight to the New Testament, and read just like the promises that God's made with you in the new covenant of His blood.

Never let anyone tell you that the old covenant doesn't prepare the way for the new covenant.

⇒ *The old covenant was made with a people which had been chosen, redeemed and adopted by the grace of God – just like you!*

⇒ *The spiritual relationship at the heart of the covenants with Noah and Abram was at the centre of God's covenant with Israel – and it's at the centre of His covenant with you!*

⇒ *God's sovereign, all-grace initiative was at the forefront of the old covenant – and it's the foundation of His new covenant with you!*

Grace and obedience

The Scriptures emphasise Israel's obedience so strongly that some leaders describe God's binding agreement with Israel as a 'covenant of law'.

But the requirements of the law that God imposed upon Israel were, *in principle*, little different to those that He'd placed upon Noah and Abram.

Israel's obligation of faith-filled obedience was not a pre-condition of the old covenant; rather, it was the means by which Israel *appropriated* and *entered into* the blessings of the binding agreement.

Some leaders teach that this covenant didn't begin until the people had promised to obey the law. But the covenant with Israel was only an adjustment of the *pre-existing* agreement with Abram, and the people had conclusive proof that God kept His covenant in their deliverance from Egypt.

The escape from Egypt shows that God's binding agreement was *already in operation*, my friend. The grace had been given and received! Israel's covenant relationship with God already existed!

This means that obedience to the law was not the way into the old covenant for Israel, it was *the way of living within the covenant*. Israel's promise of obedience was simply the only proper response to God's grace.

Moses took the Book of the Covenant and read in the hearing of the people. And they said, "All that the Lord has said we will do and be obedient".   Exodus 24:7

What does this say to you, dear friend, about the response that God is seeking from you? What is He saying to you at this moment? How are you responding to the blood of the new covenant which was shed for the remission of your sins?

⇒ *with open hands and joyful thanksgiving?*

⇒ *with careless sin so that God's grace can abound?*

⇒ *with adoring obedience?*

Although the type of obedience in the new covenant is wonderfully different from that in the old covenant, you must realise that the demand for obedience in the new covenant is, in principle, the same demand as in all the old covenants.

And, although every aspect of the new covenant is an accomplished fact through the cross, you will not enjoy the unlimited blessings of the new covenant *on earth* without loving obedience.

51

10

The messianic covenant

As well as recording God's covenants with Noah, Abraham and Israel, the Old Testament also refers to a fourth covenant – to one which God made to King David. Although the word 'covenant' is not used in the seventh chapter of 2 Samuel, it's clear that this is God's binding agreement with David.

Pick up your Bible now, dear friend, and read verses twelve to sixteen. Although, at first sight, it may seem to be referring to David's son Solomon, I'm sure it'll be plain to you that it really points to great David's greater Son, to Jesus the Messiah.

Watch out for the shadow of the cross in verse fourteen!

The prophet Isaiah often refers to this covenant with king David, and he reveals that 'the Servant' is Himself 'the covenant'.

Behold My Servant... I have put My Spirit on Him... I will keep You and give You as a covenant to the people, as a light to the Gentiles, to open blind eyes, to bring out prisoners... Isaiah 42:1-7

Under the Spirit's inspiration, Isaiah shows that all the blessings of God's covenant are bound up in this Spirit-anointed Servant, in the Messiah.

I will preserve You and give You as a covenant to the people, to restore the earth, to cause them to inherit the desolate heritages... they shall neither hunger not thirst... Isaiah 49:8-10

In fact, Isaiah reveals that the Messiah personally embodies the special relationship with God, and the blessings of God, which the covenant guarantees!

Let your soul delight itself in abundance. Incline your ear and come to Me. Hear and your soul shall live; And I will make an everlasting covenant with you – the sure mercies of David. Indeed I have given Him as a witness to the people, a leader and a commander for the people. Isaiah 55:2-4

Towards the new covenant

After reading the last few chapters of this book, my friend, you should now be in roughly the same position as the apostles at the last supper – when Jesus mentioned a new covenant in His blood.

Without needing even so much as to glance at a single page of the New Testament, you should now realise that the new covenant of God, made in Jesus' blood, will, at the very least:

⇒ *be an act of all-grace*

⇒ *provide abundant blessings*

⇒ *guarantee important promises*

⇒ *establish a holy relationship between God and His people*

⇒ *demand some form of loving obedience*

⇒ *be associated with the Spirit-anointed, sin-bearing Servant/Messiah/Christ*

Isn't it exciting when you start to see how the whole Bible fits together, and when you begin to grasp how God was preparing the way for the blood and the cross from the very dawn of time!

Doesn't it make you want to break out in praise at the greatness of God's plan! Hallelujah!

11

The new covenant

The New Testament doesn't teach that the new covenant replaced the old covenants, rather that it *fulfilled* them and brought them to fruition.

⇒ *the grace which was partially revealed in the old covenants was fully revealed and given*

⇒ *the special relationship which was partially enjoyed in the old covenants was brought to the greatest possible degree of intimacy*

⇒ *the blessings of the old covenants were developed, increased, enriched and fulfilled*

The apostle Paul writes about covenants in the book of Galatians. He explains that God's covenant with Israel did not nullify His covenant with Abram. Instead, His covenant with Israel was an *addition* which served the basic covenant promise to Abram of a special relationship between God and Abram's descendants.

Paul teaches that later covenants supplement earlier covenants, and he presents Christ as *the fulfilment* of the covenant promise made to Abram.

Although the new covenant refers *essentially* to your forgiven relationship with God (which was established through Jesus' blood on the cross), the continuity of covenants means that God's new binding agreement with you also includes

⇒ *all the grace of all the old covenants*

⇒ *all the blessing of all the old covenants*

⇒ *all the truth of all the old covenants*

⇒ *all the promises of all the old covenants*

⇒ *all the relationships of all the old covenants*

And then, my friend, the new covenant in Christ's blood promises you much, much more. Hallelujah!

The benefits of the new covenant

Paul describes some of the benefits of the new covenant in his second letter to the Corinthians.

He shows that it ministers *the Spirit of life*, that it delivers *glorious righteousness* and *absolute liberty*, and that it begins the process by which you are *transformed* into the holy image of God.

By now, dear friend, you should have grasped that, from the time of Noah until today, God's saving grace and certain blessings have always been given in the form of blood covenants.

Each successive covenant has unfolded more of God's saving will and purpose. Each covenant has always been *an enrichment* of what has always been present. And each one has been a unilateral binding agreement of grace and promise which has been set in the context of salvation.

I'm sure you already know that Calvary is the climax of grace, promise, healing, salvation and revelation; now you must grasp that the ancient covenant promise, *'I will be your God and you will be my people'*, is right at the centre of the cross.

The new covenant through Christ's blood brings this *relationship* to the highest possible level.

Quite simply, you can never receive a better promise or a more intimate relationship than that which has already been graciously provided for you by the new covenant in the shed blood of Christ!

Your faith declaration

"I confess and declare that God has established a new and unbreakable covenant with me which promises eternal forgiveness.

I affirm that Christ's blood is God's solemn pledge that He will keep His new covenant promise of forgiveness. I see the blood; I see the guarantee of my forgiveness. I'm covered with the blood; I'm covered with God's binding agreement to forgive me. Praise His covenant-keeping name!

I rejoice that God's new covenant in the blood promises me abundant blessing, and that it has bound me in a holy relationship with God.

Through the new covenant, God has provided me with glorious righteousness and absolute liberty. He has ministered the Spirit of life to me; and has started to transform me into His holy image. All the grace, blessings and promises of the old covenants are now mine through the precious blood of Christ.

I respond to your grace, dear God, with open hands and a thankful heart; and I dedicate myself to living with obedience within your new covenant.

You are my God, and I am your child. Hallelujah!"

12

The saving blood of Christ

So far, dear friend, I've been helping you to see the crimson thread which runs through the Bible, and which leads you from the Garden of Eden, through the Promised Land, straight to the cross of Christ.

You've noticed this thread in the *sacrifices* which God gave to His people, and you've noticed it in the *covenants* which He made with His people.

These Old Testament blood sacrifices and blood covenants prepared the way for the saving blood of Jesus Christ – which fulfils *everything* that the covenants and sacrifices foreshadowed.

Sacrificial blood

You've learnt that, in Egypt, the people of Israel faithfully sprinkled the blood of a sacrificial animal on the door-posts of their homes as a sign that they were God's covenant people.

When God saw the blood, He passed over the house when His judgement visited Egypt. This is why Jesus is called the 'Passover lamb', for it's through your faith in His blood that God passes over you and doesn't punish you for your sin.

You've also learnt that, on the annual Day of the Atonement, two goats were sacrificed for the guilt and sin of God's covenant people. The blood was then sprinkled on the altar as an act of atonement for the uncleanness and rebellion of the people.

In the same way, Jesus' death on the cross was the once-and-for-all atoning sacrifice for your sin. Because of His blood, you can now follow your High Priest into the holy presence of God, and can live forever in a special covenant relationship.

Covenant blood

You've also grasped that God's blood covenant with Abram is the foundation of the Christian faith, and that God has established the new covenant of Christ's blood with you on the basis of His covenant with Abram of grace, promise and faith.

The blood covenant with Abram developed the divine grace which God had already revealed in His covenant with Noah.

God laid down no conditions, and Abram offered no promises. (These came later, as God called Abram into an even closer covenant relationship and more God-like lifestyle.) The blood covenant itself was an occasion of pure grace.

In the same way, at the cross, God didn't lay down any conditions of obedience, He simply offered you *unconditional forgiveness*, promised you *new life* and guaranteed you an eternal *covenant relationship*. Your lapses and doubt can never hinder or break this covenant, for it is all all-God, it is all all-grace.

Since God made His blood covenant on the cross with you, there's been nothing more that He can do. He's made His unconditional, unilateral, everlasting promise; and the blood now witnesses to God's total sincerity and absolute faithfulness.

Rejoice, my dear friend, for the blood of the covenant now binds God to keep His Word to you for all eternity! Hallelujah!

The saving blood of Christ

Through reading this book, you've come to realise that the phrase 'the blood' refers to the complete sacrificial, covenantal death of Jesus Christ.

So now, my friend, when you celebrate the blood, make sure you remember that you're celebrating the totality of Christ's sacrificial death *and* the fullness of God's new covenant. Never forget that that Jesus' saving blood is the most important and the most valuable commodity in the universe!

The apostle Paul writes much about Jesus' saving blood in his letter to the Romans. At times, Paul uses technical words to describe some of the results of Christ's death. But here he simply states:

When we were enemies we were reconciled to God through the death of His Son, much more, having been reconciled, we shall be saved by His life.   Romans 5:10

You've learnt that the ancient covenant promise 'You shall be My people and I shall be your God' is central to the cross. Now Paul explains to you that the special relationship, which God promises in all His covenants, is *guaranteed* by the death of His Son on the cross.

My dear friend, the great, over-riding purpose of your salvation is your personal, permanent reconciliation with God. And the sacrificial blood of Jesus, shed in His faith-filled death, has fully accomplished this reconciliation and established your unbreakable covenant relationship with God.

This means that the saving blood of Jesus has performed what the old blood sacrifices could only symbolise and what the old blood covenants could only foreshadow – *eternal forgiveness from sin and absolute reconciliation with God*.

Isn't this wonderful! It's the main reason why the blood should have a very high profile in your times of praise, worship and thanksgiving!

The blood guarantees

I can hear some of you thinking that this is all well and good, that it's very interesting to learn about Adam's skins and Abram's promises, but you want to know what the blood means for you *practically*.

Don't worry, my friend, I agree! While it's important that you understand God's great plan of salvation and get to grips with His purposes, *it's even more vital* that you experience His salvation and enjoy His excellent purposes!

After all, it's no good if you can pass an exam about the crimson thread but don't experience the blood's unlimited power and blessing!

I've some good news for you, dear friend. The New Testament emphasises that the saving blood of Jesus changes *everything*, that it makes a great host of practical differences to your life!

For the next few chapters, I'm going to take you on a whistle-stop tour of the blood's practical accomplishments. I'm going to show you what the blood has done in your life, (if you're a believer) and how you can experience its *unlimited* power.

Just to whet your appetite before we begin the tour, let me tell you that, (if you're a believer) because of the precious shed blood of Christ:

⇒ *you're forgiven!*

⇒ *you're redeemed!*

⇒ *you're justified!*

⇒ *you're released from inherited bondages!*

⇒ *you're cleansed from impurity!*

⇒ *you're delivered from the law!*

⇒ *you're reconciled with God!*

⇒ *you're victorious over Satan!*

⇒ *you're sanctified!*

Christ's blood deals with *everything*, my friend – all your sin, all your guilt, all your doubts, all your weaknesses, all your failings!

Christ's first coming was all about dealing with your sin; but His second coming will have nothing to do with your sin because your forgiveness and reconciliation to God have been completed. As Jesus said on the cross, 'It's finished'!

The blood, dear friend, the blood of Christ, guarantees that you're in an utterly triumphant position over sin and guilt, over fear and bad habits, over death and demons.

The shed blood of Christ guarantees that you're a world-champion overcomer – over your past, over your present, over your future, over all evil powers.

The precious crimson thread guarantees that you're in a special, reconciled, permanent covenant relationship with God – so *nothing* can ever separate you from the love of God. Nothing at all! This is the deeply practical, covenant relationship which is yours by the blood and the cross!

Put the book down and celebrate, my friend, for *you're saved and secure for all eternity*. God's covenant with you in Christ's sacrificial blood cannot be broken. Praise His excellent name!

13

You're forgiven!

I'm sure you've noticed that the crimson thread is a thread of forgiveness. It weaves from God's gift of blood-stained clothes to the pair of sinners in Eden, through His gift of forgiveness to the people of Israel on each day of atonement, and on to His greatest gift of all through His blood on the cross.

At the last supper, Jesus declared that He would shed His blood to remit sin – to forgive all your sins, my friend, PAST, PRESENT and FUTURE!

This is My blood of the new covenant, which is shed for many for the remission of sins.
Matthew 26:28

I know that sin isn't a popular word today, but it still ruins people's lives and causes enormous pain.

Sin grips people so much that they constantly hurt themselves and damage each other by their words, thoughts, attitudes and actions. As a result of sin, lives are destroyed, families fall apart, society disintegrates, the world is polluted, and whole nations live in poverty, sickness and fear.

But we've wonderful news for the world, for the central message of our faith is that sin *has been dealt with by forgiveness* – by God remitting sin and starting the process of removing it.

Forgiveness and punishment

The crimson thread reveals that forgiveness and punishment go together. The holy love at the centre of God guarantees that anything else is impossible.

Whenever God encounters evil, He simply *must* deal with it. If He didn't punish evil in the act of forgiving sin, He wouldn't be more loving than He is, He just wouldn't be a holy God!

The Bible describes God forgiving people to such an extent that it's almost impossible for us to grasp it with our minds. Yet it also describes Him moving against sin with all the passion of His holy wrath.

The great glory of our Christian gospel is that – despite the terrible sin against which God's anger blazes – God has taken the amazing step of receiving sinful people as His intimate friends! And He's done this only because of the blood.

In Him we have redemption through His blood, the forgiveness of sins, according to the riches of His grace.   Ephesians 1:7

Perhaps, my dear friend, you're at the stage where you're still asking yourself some of these questions.

⇒ *Will I ever be clean from this sin?*

⇒ *How can I ever be really forgiven?*

⇒ *Must I always bear this terrible burden?*

⇒ *Can nothing bring me close to God?*

⇒ *Will I always feel this aching pain and loneliness?*

⇒ *Can I ever be free from the habits and memories which bind me?*

You may be ashamed of some episodes in your past. You may wish that you could forget what you've done. Remember the crimson thread, my friend! The blood of Christ has done everything for you – it *guarantees* your forgiveness!

68

Of course, you still have to restore anything you've stolen and try to repair any broken human relationships. But, through the blood, God has dealt with *all* your sin. Like the goat driven into the wilderness, He has driven your sin so far away that He cannot see it or remember it any more. You're clean in His sight! You're spotless and holy! You're forgiven!

You may find it hard to believe that God has forgiven your worst sin. But that's the *unlimited* power of the blood. No matter what you've done or thought, the blood has dealt with it all!

The reality of God's forgiveness is so great that it can't be explained to someone who's not experienced it. You won't reach forgiveness by thinking about it, dear friend, you must simply be confronted by the blood on the cross!

The crimson thread of forgiveness comes to you straight from God as an unexplainable gift which contains the solution to *all* your problems.

Once you accept this gift, you can endure the weight of your problems and put things right with people without complaining – because you know that God has forgiven you. He is your covenant friend, and has provided everything that you need.

14

You're redeemed!

When Jesus died on the cross, He willingly accepted the responsibility for *all* your sin. In fact, He took the blame for every wrong that's been committed throughout human history – past, present and future!

On the cross, Jesus accepted liability for all the hurt, harm, suffering, pain, selfishness, sickness, sin, sorrow, evil and guilt that has occurred, and that will occur. This reveals His unlimited love.

Of His own free will, Jesus chose to endure the punishment which you deserve so that you need *never* endure your righteous punishment. He's borne it all for you! Hallelujah!

Sin covered and carried away

I expect you know that the Old Testament talks about sin being 'covered' – rather like you might place a rug over a stain on your carpet so that visitors can't see the dirty mark.

Sin is always a direct challenge to God, and, in the Old Testament, it was covered by the shedding of blood. As you know, on the Day of Atonement the sacrifice of two goats both covered the sins of God's people and carried them far away.

Through their blood, God dealt with sin temporarily. And, on the cross, Jesus' blood *completed* what the animals' blood had begun. When His blood had drained from His body, it had covered your sins and carried them eternally away!

At that moment, *everything changed*. A new age began – the age of salvation and forgiveness!

The ransom

Everyone knows about the powerful grip of sin. I'm sure there's been much good that you've wanted to do but haven't done. And that there's been many wrong deeds which you just couldn't stop yourself doing. Despite all your good intentions, my friend, you were held captive by sin.

71

The Bible describes this condition by saying that men and women are 'slaves to sin'. It's as though they've been *kidnapped* by sin and cannot get free: they need someone who'll pay a ransom to the kidnappers to purchase their freedom.

Praise God, for this is exactly what Jesus did on the cross! He paid the ransom which bought your freedom – He redeemed you with His blood!

You were not redeemed with corruptible things, like silver and gold... but with the precious blood of Christ.   1 Peter 1:18-19

Just like slaves, prisoners-of-war and kidnap victims, you were held in a captivity from which you could be released only by the payment of a price, by a *ransom*.

You would have died in captivity if the ransom hadn't been paid. But Jesus eagerly paid your ransom with the most valuable commodity in the universe, with His life-blood, and so you are free.

Purchased with a price

Some believers concentrate on the great victory that Jesus won over Satan at the cross. But Jesus didn't defeat Satan by force. He didn't smash him into submission with superior power. Rather, Jesus conquered Satan by perfect goodness and absolute obedience to the Father.

It's important you realise, my friend, that Jesus didn't rescue you from sin by twisting Satan's arm to release you. Instead, He rescued you by doing the right thing, by purchasing you with His blood, by paying the prescribed price.

If Jesus had tried to use force (one of Satan's weapons) the devil would have gained a fingerhold and frustrated your salvation.

Yet, despite everything that the devil did at the cross, he could gain no hold on Jesus. And, when Jesus shed His blood without sin, the devil had to concede defeat and release you from captivity.

The price had been paid. You were no longer his. You had a new owner. You'd been bought by Jesus. You belonged completely to Him! The blood had done its work! Hallelujah!

This is very, very practical. Jesus died to set you free from *all* the ravages of sin, sickness and wickedness, from *all* the pain and restrictions of sin, from *all* the evil habits you've inherited from your ancestors.

However, in paying the ransom price by His blood, Jesus not only earnt your release, He also bought you for Himself.

You're not your own, my friend! You've been bought with the blood! You were a slave of sin; now you're a slave of Christ. You were in the grip of sin; now you're in the strong grip of God.

This changes everything!

Look around you: every believer you see illustrates the unlimited power of the blood. Every single believer has been released from sin *by the blood*. Every one has been lovingly purchased *with the blood*. Every one can live in victory and holiness *through the blood*. It's unlimited power changes everything!

Unlimited power!

Do you remember those pictures a few years ago of the Beirut hostages. Many were released quickly because their governments met the kidnappers' demands for money and arms.

But men like Terry Waite and John McCarthy were held in terrible conditions for many years because the British government wouldn't deal with their captors.

74

When the hostages were finally released, they had to learn to live in freedom. They'd become so used to chains and beatings, to their way of living in captivity, that they found it hard to enjoy the blessings of freedom.

It's rather similar for believers. The ransom has been paid. We have been redeemed. But, after our long years of captivity, we often slip back into the old habits of sin.

In fact, some believers live in their blood-bought freedom as if they were still held in captivity. They are genuine slaves of God, but they act as if they were still slaves of sin.

Don't be like them, dear friend. If you trust the blood, it's unlimited power can produce practical results in you which are far, far greater than anything you've yet experienced.

Through your faith in the blood of Christ, you can enjoy your freedom. Strengthen your faith now by recognising what the blood has already accomplished in your life – and by claiming those great covenant promises which guarantee that God will provide you with everything you need, including your healing.

15

You're justified!

Over the years, I've listened to hundreds of people who've been struggling to enjoy their blood-bought blessings and freedom.

They know that they've been saved. They trust God and believe the Bible. They've been baptised in water and filled with the Holy Spirit. They're regular in worship and pray in tongues.

But they're struggling. Something's stopping them from enjoying God and living in hope and victory.

It's their past!

It seems to me that more and more believers are spiritually depressed. They may hide this at meetings behind their smiles. They may insist that they're 'fine' when somebody greets them. But on the inside, they're spiritually weak and tired.

You might not be spiritually paralysed, my friend, but you've a few weaknesses and you've made some mistakes – we all have. Satan knows them, and he uses our past mistakes to try to depress us and to stop us from enjoying our freedom.

Let me ask you two questions.

⇒ *What would you say if I asked you to list your three worst sins?*

⇒ *What would God say if you asked Him to identify your three worst sins?*

The truth, dear friend, is that, even though you might remember your past misdeeds, GOD DOES NOT! He's wiped your slate clean. He's declared you 'not guilty'. He's justified you by the blood!

Much more then, having been justified by His blood, we shall be saved from wrath through Him.   Romans 5:9

Some people think that their pasts are particularly bad, and that other believers wouldn't have any time for them if they knew what they'd done.

77

But nobody is worse than anyone else when we're all compared to God's holiness. With God, sin is missing the target of His absolute perfection, and 'a miss is as good as a mile' when we miss a target!

According to God's standards, one sin bears exactly the same consequence as a million sins. This means that *everyone is equally sinful*, and that all people are in equal need of forgiveness.

If you could see your past as God once saw it, my friend, before He applied the blood, you'd realise that your past was as black as black could be.

But the moment He applied the blood to your life, all your sin was covered and carried away. Your misdeeds have gone forever and they CANNOT be remembered or recalled by God.

Frankly, my dear friend, we insult and defame the precious blood of Christ every time that we think about one of our past sins.

You're not guilty!

The Bible often uses the technical word 'justified', and this has to do with justice. It describes what happens when the Judge of all the world declares sinners 'not guilty' and acquits them of *all* the charges against them.

If you've never sinned, you won't need to face the holy Judge, or you'll be confident of acquittal. But, because of your sin, you know that you're guilty and that you deserve to be punished.

However, because of the blood, which has covered your sins and carried them away, you can be certain that God will declare you 'not guilty'.

The Judge has announced that you're free from all liability for your sins – even from those 'worst' sins which seem to haunt your memories and paralyse your spiritual service.

The Judge has made this declaration because God-in-Christ, through the blood, has borne the penalty for your sin – *even for sin which haunts your memories and paralyses your service.*

Remember this my dear friend.

⇒ You're justified *by God*. Embrace this verdict right now. Receive it and believe it by faith.

⇒ You're justified *in Christ*. You're joined to Him, so God sees Him when He looks at you.

⇒ You're justified *through the blood*. Its great power has saved you from God's holy wrath.

It's just like the Garden of Eden! When God forgave you, He stripped you of all the filthy

79

clothes of your sin and self-effort. Then, when He justified you, He clothed you with the blood-stained clothes of Christ so that you could serve Him in the world and the church.

I am He who blots out your transgressions for My own sake. I will not remember your sins. Put Me in remembrance; let us contend together; state your case, that you may be acquitted.   Isaiah 43:25-26

If you're still troubled by the memory of a past sin, dear friend, you need to repent for not believing God's covenant promise.

Stop listening to your emotions! Stop listening to those evil thoughts which try to convince you that you're no good! Start believing the Word!

In Him we have redemption through His blood, the forgiveness of sins, according to the riches of His grace.   Ephesians 1:7

Claim God's blood promise now. Speak out the *fact* of your forgiveness. Declare the *fact* of your redemption. Announce the *fact* of your justification.

It's really true, my friend, the unlimited power of the blood has dealt with your sin. Now it's time that you started really to believe it – and to live it!

80

16

You're reconciled!

When you look at the people around you, it should be plain that men and women have been made for relationships. From the moment of your birth, my friend, you've lived your life in an ever-changing network of human relationships.

Friends, family, neighbours, colleagues – I'm sure that they all matter deeply to you. If you're like most people, you'll want to be recognised, acknowledged, valued and loved; and you'll long to experience genuine, lasting, committed friendships.

Although more people in Western Europe now live on their own, nobody's meant to live in complete isolation. Modern societies reserve the punishment of solitary confinement for their most dangerous criminals!

The truth is that there's something about human beings which causes us to long for loving relationships and to ache over broken relationships. I'm sure you've already discovered, dear friend, that there's little which hurts as much as the pain of a family break-up or a rift with a close friend.

Sin and reconciliation

Broken relationships are always caused by some sort of sin – which is why they're so hard to mend. When you start to feel envious of someone, or to gossip about them, or to speak sharply to them, you're bound to become distanced from them.

However, the same sinful thought or action which causes a small rift between you and a friend, also causes a mighty chasm between you and God.

Sin always has a greater effect on the all-holy God than on its human victims. They might feel able to try to overlook the sin – whereas God, in His absolute holiness, can *never* ignore a sin. He must act against it with His righteous judgement.

Although sin usually separates people from each other, it always isolates them from God. Because of the effect of their sin *on God*, people have to live in the spiritual equivalent of solitary confinement. This is why so many people feel distant from God.

Of course, just as people ache for their broken human relationships to be restored, so they instinctively long for *ultimate reconciliation*. Not everyone recognises this yearning for what it is; even so, most people respond to it subconsciously by searching for some sort of spiritual relationship.

God and reconciliation

At every level, reconciliation is impossible until the wronged party will overlook the sin which caused the rift. When you wrong someone, my friend, you cannot insist on being reconciled – it's up to them.

In the same way, the holy God – who has been so terribly sinned against – is the only one who can bring about ultimate reconciliation. Praise Him, for this is exactly what He's done on the cross!

All things are of God, who has reconciled us to Himself through Jesus Christ, and has given us the ministry of reconciliation, that is, that God was in Christ reconciling the world to Himself...
2 Corinthians 5:18-19

83

God has reconciled you to Him

You've learnt, dear friend, that the new covenant in the blood is about a special relationship with God.

As a creature made by the Creator, you were brought into being for this special relationship. But you've quarrelled with God; you've insisted on your own way; you've said 'No!' to God; and so the relationship has been broken. Sadly, because of your sin, you became one of God's enemies.

However, through the blood on the cross, God has fully and eternally reconciled you with Him.

By the power of the blood, God has torn down the barrier between you; He's bridged the chasm; He's repaired the relationship which existed before Adam's sin – and it can *never* be breached again!

Because of the blood, my dear friend,

⇒ *you're at peace with God!*

⇒ *you've access to God!*

⇒ *you're one with God!*

⇒ *you're adopted by God!*

⇒ *you're right with God!*

⇒ *you're reconciled with God!*

Praise His wonderful name!

17

You're saved - by faith!

None of the things that we've considered in the last few chapters are mere 'arm-chair' theories.

Forgiveness isn't an idea for you only to turn over in your mind!

Redemption isn't a subject for you just to discuss at your house-group!

Justification isn't a topic for you simply to make notes about!

Reconciliation isn't a matter for idle debate!

No! These are practical, life-changing realities which you must experience, embrace and enjoy.

The unlimited power of the blood won't make any difference to your life, my friend, unless you:

⇒ *receive the gift that God offers you*

⇒ *accept what Jesus has achieved for you*

⇒ *claim the power of the blood*

⇒ *hunger and thirst for righteousness, and for all the blessings of your special covenant relationship (healing, provision, the Holy Spirit, and so on)*

Although forgiveness, redemption, justification and reconciliation are free gifts from God, there's nothing mechanical or automatic about them.

It's not inevitable that all human beings will be forgiven, and it's not inevitable that you'll experience the fullness of God's covenant blessings! You must do something to realise and unwrap all the gifts of the blood.

When the crowds on the day of Pentecost asked Peter what they should do, he told them:

Repent, and let every one of you be baptised in the name of Jesus Christ for the remission of sins; and you shall receive the gift of the Holy Spirit.   Acts 2:38

Peter didn't say that there was nothing for them to do. He didn't say that God had done everything, so they could go home without doing anything. But, equally, he didn't suggest that they had to do something which would earn them the promised blessings or create the remission of their sin.

Repent

Let me ask you some important questions.

⇒ *Do you need to be forgiven, redeemed, justified and reconciled?*

The first step on the way to experiencing the unlimited power of the blood is to be aware that – before you can be fully healthy and whole – you must be forgiven, redeemed, and so on.

⇒ *Do you need to be forgiven by God?*

Do you think that the wrong you've done needs to be dealt with only by the people you've hurt? Or are you aware just how much you've hurt God?

The second step is to recognise that you need to be forgiven, justified, and so on, by God Himself.

⇒ *Can you do anything about your sin?*

Can you? Can you handle your life on your own? Resolve your problems? Deal with your sin?

87

The third step of repentance is recognising that you're a slave to sin, and that there's nothing you can do about it.

⇒ *Can God do anything about your sin?*

Can He? Is all our talk about the blood relevant to your life? Or are you so unimportant that God can't be bothered with you?

The final step of repentance is realising that God has done everything necessary to forgive you, to redeem you, to justify you and to reconcile you with Himself.

Believe

You were saved, dear friend, by Jesus, through the blood that He shed on the cross. But you can practically experience this salvation only by faith.

God is holding forgiveness, reconciliation, and so on, out to you. But you've got to grab hold of them – that's faith!

You don't need much faith. You don't need to make a superhuman effort. You simply have to believe that Jesus has earnt your full salvation.

You don't need to understand everything in this book; you merely have to believe enough in

Jesus to ask Him to save you and to accept what He offers you.

Nothing physical will happen to your body when you believe, for you're dealing with facts, not feelings.

The fact is that, because of the blood, God in Christ has forgiven you, has redeemed you, has justified you, and has reconciled you with Himself.

Do you believe this fact, my friend? If your answer is 'Yes', then you've responded to the blood with faith. But if you're still not quite sure, you've not responded with faith.

Whoever believes in Him will receive remission of sins.   Acts 10:43

Baptism

The Apostle Peter told the Pentecost crowd that they must be baptised in the name of Jesus for the remission of sins. This teaching is often repeated in the New Testament.

Why are you waiting? Arise and be baptised, and wash away your sins, calling on the name of the Lord.   Acts 22:16

Of course, God doesn't tie His blood gifts to any rite or ceremony. But the repentant believer who is baptised in the name of Jesus can know *for certain* that their sins have been completely and eternally removed, that they're safe in the special covenant relationship.

Baptism without repentance and faith cannot result in salvation, but it's foolish to ignore the New Testament teaching and think that baptism is pointless or unnecessary.

Forgiveness, redemption, justification and reconciliation are unconditional covenant gifts from God *to you*. There's nothing that you can do to earn them, my dear friend, but you really do need to unwrap them – by faith in Christ and baptism in water.

Only then will you really start to enjoy and experience the unlimited power of the blood.

18

You're cleansed!

By far the most important effect of the blood on your life, dear friend, is your total reconciliation with God Himself.

Once you were His enemy; now you are His covenant friend and child. Once you could not dare to approach Him; now you live in His presence. Once you were paralysed by guilt and fear; now you're fully at peace with your Lord and Maker.

But the power of the blood of Christ doesn't stop operating once you're reconciled with God. Far from it! The power of the blood is *unlimited*, it keeps working in your life long *after* you've been born again.

As you go on yielding to the Holy Spirit, as you keep on living in the light, as you continue to respond with faith to God's Word, so the blood works ever more deeply in your life and imparts more of God's covenant blessings to you.

In the next few chapters, I'm going to describe some of the ways that the blood keeps on working in the lives of believers. One of the most important blessings of the blood is *cleansing from sin*.

Many believers think that cleansing occurs only at conversion. But the Bible teaches that we need 'initial' cleansing when we first turn to God *and* that we also need 'on-going' cleansing throughout our earthly life.

If we walk in the light as He is in the light, we have fellowship with one another, and the blood of Jesus Christ His Son cleanses us from all sin. 1 John 1:7

Cleansing (some versions of the Bible call it *purifying*) refers to the blood's work in dealing with all the polluting effects of sin.

The blood removes the filth of sin; it washes away the defilement which gathers on our lives through our own sin and through our contact with the sinful world around us.

Many believers know that their sins have been forgiven, yet they're still troubled by memories of their sins. They need the blood to wash away the stain of their sin. Does this apply to you, my friend?

If we confess our sins, He is faithful and just to forgive us our sins and to cleanse us from all unrighteousness.   1 John 1:9

And I'm sure that you've felt the grime of sin on your soul after overhearing somebody swear, or seeing an unclean television programme, or feeling the world's greed. Most evenings, we all need a good wash in the blood to get rid of the filth that we've picked up just by being in the world!

Practical cleansing

Let me take you through four steps of cleansing.

1. First, you need to *know* that you can be clean. God will not only cover your sin with the blood, He will also cleanse you from sin with the blood.

   You don't need to know how God wipes away the stain of sin to give you a clear conscience and trouble free thoughts, you just need to know that He will do this and that He wills to do this.

2. Second, you must *hunger and thirst* to be clean. You must want to be holy more than you want anything else. You must ache to be God-like.

Remember, God will grant the desires of your heart, so make holiness your strongest desire.

3. Third, you must be willing to *separate yourself* from everything which is dirty or unclean.

You must be ready for every aspect of your life to be baptised in the blood – your relationships and possessions, your hopes and ambitions, your habits and attitudes, your hobbies and ideas, your memories and desires, and so on.

4. Finally, you must *exercise faith* in the unlimited power of the blood.

Unbelief hinders the blood's power in your life, but faith removes this blockage and opens your heart for the cleansing power to work.

Claim it now

God's Word promises that the blood will cleanse you from sin. Claim it now! Claim it every day! Don't start the next chapter until you've spent time asking Jesus to wash you in His blood and to wipe away the defilement that's gathered in your life. His blood really will cleanse you from *all* sin.

19

You're released!

God has reconciled you with Himself through the blood, my friend, so that you can live for ever in the special relationship He's planned for you.

When He drew you to Himself by the Spirit, and you responded to His grace with living faith, you were instantly redeemed, forgiven, justified and reconciled – all because of the blood on the cross.

But this was not the end of the blood's power, for it continues to operate in your life as you go on responding to God with faith and loving obedience.

By now, you should know that God wants to keep on using the blood to scrub you clean from every stain of sin. But even this deep cleansing is not the end of the blood's power, for God also wants to keep on using the blood to release you from:

⇒ *the grip of the law*

⇒ *the grip of inherited bondages*

⇒ *the grip of Satan*

Can I hear some of you saying that you thought God had released you from these things at conversion?

Is this so, my friend? Are you honestly saying that – since you were converted – you've never been troubled by legalistic thoughts, or by old patterns of behaviour which were passed down to you from your parents and grandparents, or even by Satan?

Remember, we're not discussing vague theories in this book, we're concerned with practical realities.

If you think that something should have changed within you at conversion, and you know that – deep inside yourself – it hasn't changed very much, you'll eventually start to doubt your conversion!

You need to be clear in your mind what God *has done once-and-for-all* through the blood, and what He wants to *keep on doing* through the blood.

He *has* forgiven you. He *has* justified you. He *has* redeemed you. He *has* fully reconciled you. These are absolute facts which nothing can change.

God did all these things for you at the cross so that you could live in a special covenant relationship with Him. And now that you're in this position of intimacy with God, He wants to keep on delivering you from the grip of the law, and from every form of evil.

Cleansing from sin

It's rather like you've taken a very bad tumble on a muddy, gritty road, and are dazed, grazed, bruised, bleeding and dirty.

God wants to take you in His arms, gently to wash away the defilement of sin, carefully to cleanse your wounds, and lovingly to apply the balm which will bring your complete healing.

God doesn't go on cleansing you in this way with the blood, my friend, just so that you can approach Him for the first time.

Rather, He keeps on cleansing you in this way – like good parents keep on caring for their children – because of the committed, covenant relationship that He's established with you through the blood.

97

Release from evil

And it's also rather like you've been pushed into a thick clump of brambles, and are struggling to pull yourself free from the long, thorny stems which are gripping you tight.

God wants you to call to Him, dear friend, like a child calls to its parents, and to trust Him to cut the brambles away from your life so that you can live in His blessing and freedom.

Once again, God doesn't release you from these things just so that you can approach Him for the first time. Instead, He wants to release you *every time* you become entangled – because you're His child, because He's totally committed to your welfare, because of His new covenant with you in the precious blood of Christ.

Claiming the promised land

As a believer, you're called to live in the tension between knowing that the blood has made you free in Christ *and* that you need to keep on appropriating this freedom in your daily experience.

Your struggles with the enemy must not make you doubt your freedom. And the truth of the cross must not make you complacent about applying it!

The Scriptures make it plain that:

Christ redeemed us from the curse of the law by becoming a curse for us.   Galatians 3:13

You were redeemed from the empty way of life handed down to you from your forefathers... with the precious blood of Christ. 1 Peter 1:18-19

By His death He might destroy him who holds the power of death – that is, the devil.   Hebrews 2:14

Never forget, dear friend, that Christ did defeat Satan on the cross through His obedient death; He did earn your redemption from the law; He did redeem you from inherited bondages.

But these are covenant blessings, my friend, which you need actively to keep claiming by faith throughout your life *if you're to go on experiencing the blood's unlimited power in your life.*

Remember, even though God gave the children of Israel the promised land of Canaan, they still had to fight every inch of the way to possess it and to enjoy its abundant blessings.

In a similar way, God has given you the blood-bought covenant blessings of release from the law, release from inherited bondages and release from

99

evil (and many, many more blessings on top which guarantee healing, peace, provision, and so on), but you need to keep on claiming them with living faith if you're to experience them practically in your life.

Let me ask you a few personal questions.

⇒ *Do you have any special rules which you think God wants you to try to keep?*

For example, do you think that God wants you to pray at a certain time and in a particular way; to reject certain foods or beverages, to adopt certain postures in worship, to use special words and phrases when you are talking to God or about God?

⇒ *Are you repeating the mistakes, habits, or sicknesses of your parents or ancestors?*

For example, are you troubled by something like alcoholism, immorality, divorce or criminal activity – just like your mother or father before you. Or are you struggling with something like your grandfather's bad temper or your great-uncle's problem with gambling?

⇒ *Do you find yourself giving in to the same temptation again and again and again?*

For example, do you find it almost impossible to resist the temptation to fall into debt, to lust after people in your secret thoughts, to pass on gossip, to speak little 'white' lies, and so on?

Total release

The good news, dear friend, is that you've been released from all these things by the perfect blood of Jesus.

But it's not enough to know this fact intellectually. If you want to experience total release in your life you must keep on laying hold of everything that the blood has done for you *by faith*.

This usually involves real spiritual warfare, and it isn't always easy. You may have to take a very strong stand against the law, or against inherited tendencies, or against the evil one.

You will have to stand firm in your covenant position in Christ; but if you keep on claiming your blood-bought freedom, and if you keep on resisting the devil's suggestions, you will start to experience total release from the enemy's efforts to enslave you in some form of fear or bondage.

Remember what you learnt in the last chapter. The same spiritual principles which applied to your cleansing also apply to your release.

1. You need to *know* that you can be released from whatever is holding you back. God will not only cleanse you with the blood, He will also use the blood to set you free.

2. You must *hunger and thirst* to be released. You must want to be holy more than you want anything else. You must ache to be God-like.

3. You must be willing to *separate yourself* from everything which is holding you back.

4. You must *exercise faith* in the unlimited power of the blood.

Please don't turn the page, my friend, until you've done business with God. We're all affected in some way by the law, our ancestors and the devil, but the blood's unlimited power means that *every* believer can experience total release.

Ask God to reveal how you are affected, and then start to claim your total freedom in the precious blood of Christ.

The Bible promises you victory because of the blood – don't settle for anything less!

20

You're sanctified!

So far, my dear friend, we've thought mainly about the way that God uses Jesus' precious blood to deal with your old life.

By now, you should have grasped that God wants to use the blood's unlimited power to cleanse you fully from every stain of sin and to release you completely from every form of evil.

But this is mere preparation!

God also wants to sanctify you with the blood, and this is the real meat of your Christian life, the real on-going work of the blood. God wants to bless you with sanctification, to bless you with holiness – so that you become like Christ Himself.

Therefore Jesus also, that He might sanctify the people with His own blood, suffered outside the gate.   Hebrews 13:12

Once again, sanctification isn't something which occurs instantly and completely at conversion.

God's doesn't want to sanctify you so that you can approach Him with immunity just for the first time. Rather, He longs to keep on sanctifying you, to keep on shaping you into His own likeness, because of your covenant relationship.

Holiness

Sanctification isn't an everyday word any more, and most new believers don't have a clue what it means.

Quite simply, sanctification is the process by which God makes you holy, by which He makes you like Himself.

God's holiness isn't His hostility to sin, it's *the sum total of all His attributes*. When you add together God's love, joy, faith, justice, power, goodness, and so on, the result is His holiness.

Because of this holiness, God always is, and always wills, and always does, what is utterly good. This guarantees that He always wants the utterly good in-and-for all His creatures, even for you my friend, even for you!

God wants *you* to be as holy as Him because He knows that this is the very best thing that could happen to you.

Of course, it's impossible for you to become holy by trying to be holy! You can become holy only by receiving God's holiness, by receiving Him Himself.

If you want this to happen, you must develop your intimate, covenant relationship with God, and be totally dedicated to Him and to all His ways.

Nevertheless, God's Word also encourages you to sanctify yourself.

Be holy, for I am holy.   1 Peter 1:16

God is committed to developing an intimate covenant *partnership* with you, and He will not cleanse you or release you or sanctify you against your will. You can't make yourself holy without God, and He won't make you holy without your full agreement!

Just as you've learnt to receive your cleansing and release by faith, so too you must surrender yourself completely to God to receive His holiness – for it's only the presence of God which can bring about His holiness.

Sanctification by the blood

God's greatest single purpose for you, my friend, is that you will fully participate in His holiness. This, therefore, is the single main reason why Jesus suffered and died on the cross. Quite simply, He shed His blood so that He might sanctify you.

In Gethsemane, the night before He was to die on the cross, Jesus told the Father that:

For their sakes I sanctify Myself, that they also may be sanctified by the truth.   John 17:19

Jesus sanctified Himself by committing Himself totally to the Father's will – even though it meant shedding His blood on the cross. And He did this so that you can be sanctified, so that you can receive God's holy nature and become holy.

I can't overstate how important it is, my friend, for you to grasp that your sanctification is the chief purpose of all Christ's sufferings.

106

Jesus shed His blood so that you can be holy. Your forgiveness, justification, redemption, reconciliation, cleansing and release are all very important. But they're not ends in themselves. Rather, they point forwards to the ultimate goal of your godliness, of your holiness, of your sanctification.

Too many Christians are so full of praise at their salvation that they miss the purpose of their salvation and do not press on to the goal. Don't be like them, my friend! Don't settle for some of the blood's power. Press God for everything!

Be sanctified

I'm sure you know now that God has bought you for Himself with the blood. He wants you to belong entirely to Him. He's chosen you to be His child. He's set you apart to live with Him, and with Him alone.

This setting apart, or *separation*, is the beginning of your sanctification. You've been bought with the blood, dear friend, and have been set aside for God.

Now you must live in this state of separation and surrender yourself fully to living only in-and-for God's holy will.

Don't be daunted by this task, for – in its unlimited power – the blood exists to sanctify you.

The blood represents Jesus' consecration to the cross and His complete self-surrender to God's will. This means that the closer you come to the blood, and the more that you're aware of being sprinkled by the blood, the louder you'll hear the blood calling you to devote yourself to God.

The blood is calling you closer and closer to God, my friend. It's telling you that heaven is wide-open to you, that you've free access to God, that God is beckoning you into His presence.

The blood has made it possible for you to enjoy a special, intimate relationship with God. As you surrender yourself to the blood's power, to its cleansing and release, so you'll grow in confidence that God will give Himself fully to you and will fill you with His holiness.

Are you willing to lose everything? Are you eager to say goodbye to everything, to surrender all that you hold dear, so that Jesus may sanctify you?

If you really are willing to experience the power of the blood, and if you sincerely long to be holy, you can be 100% certain that you will be sanctified by Jesus, through His blood.

You've now come to the end of our short tour of the blood's practical accomplishments. Before you move on to the next section, pause here to make your response to the blood's unlimited power.

Your faith declaration

"I affirm and declare that the living God has forgiven all my sins, past, present and future, through the precious blood of Christ.

I confess that His blood has done everything I need. Its unlimited power has changed everything.

Through the precious blood, God has paid the price of my guilt, borne the penalty of my wrongdoing, redeemed me from captivity, cleansed me from impurity, released me from inherited bondages, delivered me from the grip of Satan and the law, declared me not guilty, purchased me for Himself, set me apart for His special purposes, torn down the barrier between us, and repaired our broken relationship.

I receive these gifts. I accept these gifts. I depend on these gifts. I am hungry for God's holiness and am willing to be changed.

Because of the blood's great power, I am at peace with God. I am His and He is mine. Hallelujah!"

21

The blood speaks to you

At the end of the last chapter, I suggested that the blood is speaking to you, urging you deeper into God's presence.

Some of you may have been puzzled by this, and may have found it difficult to imagine how you could ever hear blood speak.

It's picture language, my friend!

A man or woman can look across a room at another person, and – without literally speaking – the smile or frown on their face can 'speak' volumes. The other person knows exactly what the first person is wanting to 'say' to them.

It's much the same in many areas of life. I'm sure you've said that you've been 'moved' by a piece of music when you haven't actually moved an inch!

Many parents keep their children's first paintings, and – decades later – these childish scribbles help them to recall real events and times of great happiness. In itself, a drawing is dead and dumb; nevertheless, it can act as a sign which 'speaks' to the parents and reminds them of the days when their children were small.

When we say that the blood which was shed on the cross still speaks to believers today, we don't mean that the blood somehow manages to gurgle an audible sentence which we hear with our physical ears!

Instead, we mean that the blood is a permanent sign which acts as a reminder, as a revelation, as a guarantee of some deep and profound truth which is associated with the cross.

In the next few chapters, I'm going to show you what the blood is still 'saying' to you. From now on, whenever you think or speak or sing about the precious blood, you can be sure that God is reminding you about what He's done for you – and what He still longs to do in you and through you.

The blood assures you of God's love

The first sentence that the blood speaks to you, my friend, is 'God loves you!'

The shed blood of Christ is your eternal assurance of God's love. It proves that God loves you so much that He gave His only Son to die for you.

The Bible always defines God's love in terms of the cross. For example:

God demonstrates His own love towards us, in that while we were still sinners, Christ died for us.
Romans 5:8

By this we know love, because He laid down His life for us.
1 John 3:16

At the cross, the Son died, stretched by soldiers between thieves, and His blood poured from His wounded, broken body.

Why? Because of the love of the Father and the Son and the Spirit for you, my friend. It was God's precious gift of life to you, His beloved friend.

Since the cross of Calvary, you simply cannot look at the blood and question God's love with any integrity, because nothing could demonstrate God's love more clearly to you than this self-sacrifice.

Sprinkle the blood on your doubts

My dear friend, it's likely that you'll have to face some testing circumstances soon which may prompt you to doubt God's love.

The pressures and difficulties of modern life are a stern test of faith. Matters like redundancy, unemployment, debt, family break-up, illness, and so on, can tempt believers to question God's personal love.

In the future, when you catch yourself wondering about God's great love for you, remember to sprinkle the blood on your doubts.

In faith, cover your difficult circumstances with the blood so that the truth of God's love overwhelms your doubts.

The blood won't make your circumstances go away! But *it will provide you with such a deep assurance of God's love* that you'll be able to endure your circumstances and overcome them with godly patience.

22

The blood guarantees
the new covenant

Back in chapter eight, you learnt that Christ's blood is God's solemn pledge to you that He will keep all His new covenant promises.

This means the second sentence that the blood speaks to you is, 'God will keep His covenant'.

When you see the blood, dear friend, you see:

⇒ *the guarantee of your forgiveness*

⇒ *the guarantee of your redemption*

⇒ *the guarantee of your justification*

⇒ *the guarantee of your reconciliation*

⇒ *the guarantee of your cleansing*

⇒ *the guarantee of your release*

⇒ *the guarantee of your sanctification*

Whenever you think about the blood, dear friend, allow it to remind you that God has bound Himself *unconditionally* to provide you with all these amazing covenant blessings. It's the gospel! It's almost too good to be true! Hallelujah!

The covenant with Abraham

Do you remember that, when God made His blood covenant with Abram, it was as though He was saying, 'Let me be as these broken pieces of animals if I fail to keep My Word to you.'?

In the same way, the blood is 'saying' to you that God has pledged – as solemnly, seriously and finally as possible – to keep His promises to you of covenant salvation, covenant blessing and covenant relationship.

This is the covenant I will make with the house of Israel: after those days, says the Lord, I will put My laws in their minds and write them on their hearts. I will be their God, and they shall be My people. Hebrews 8:10

In the story of Abraham, the blood was God's gracious response to Abraham's request for a token of assurance. Although Abraham was clearly 'in faith', he still had some doubts.

I expect that you're rather similar to Abraham. You've responded to God with living faith. You love God and are a genuine believer. But you're still troubled by the occasional doubt.

Perhaps you sometimes ask yourself:

⇒ *How do I know it's going to happen?*

⇒ *How can I be sure that I'll gain all this?*

God's response to your doubts, my friend, is the same as His response to Abraham. It's the blood!

When your faith starts to flag, and you wonder if God will ever get round to providing you with what He's promised, remember to listen to the blood, for it binds God to keep His Word to you.

Because of the blood, God's covenant with you *cannot* be broken.

Drench your doubts with the blood, dear friend. Do it now! Bathe in the absolute certainty of God's blood-guaranteed covenant provision.

23

The blood provides certain victory

When you look in the mirror each morning, my friend, what do you see? A six stone spiritual weakling? Or a world champion overcomer?

Are you the sort of believer who flinches when the evil one whistles in your direction? Or are you an all-conquering hero whose rippling spiritual muscles bring fear to the kingdom of darkness?

Maybe you're neither an out-and-out weakling nor quite a champion overcomer. Perhaps you feel mildly strong on some days, while at other times you feel rather weak. Is this what it's like for you?

No! No! No! A thousand times, No!

Your victory doesn't depend on your feelings, my friend, it depends on the blood! For it's the blood which places you in a victorious position over all the works of the enemy.

The blood's third vital sentence to you is, 'You're much more than a conqueror – through Him who loved you'.

Who is he that condemns? Christ Jesus, who died – more than that, who was raised to life – is at the right hand of God and is also interceding for us.

Who shall separate us from the love of Christ? Shall trouble or hardship or persecution or famine or nakedness or danger or sword?...

No, in all these things we are more than conquerors through Him who loved us. For I am convinced that neither death nor life, nor angels nor demons, neither the present nor the future, nor any powers, neither height nor depth, nor anything else in creation, will be able to separate us from the love of God that is Jesus Christ our Lord.   Romans 8:34-39 (NIV)

Do you know how to become an overcomer, my friend? Do you know how to deal with the enemy's weapons of suffering, self-condemnation, lies and deception? Do you know how to cope with all the trouble and hardship of life in a fallen world?

As usual, God's Word contains the answer:

They overcame him by the blood of the Lamb and by the word of their testimony; they did not love their lives so much as to shrink from death.

Revelation 12:11 (NIV)

This doesn't mean that you should throw blood at a problem like a robber throws acid at a victim!

Rather, it means the blood reminds you of the truth that Satan was decisively defeated at the cross by Christ's willing obedience to death.

On the cross, the devil provoked Jesus through torture, injustice, lies and insults; but Jesus refused to retaliate. He could have summoned an army of angels to help him. He could even have stepped down from the cross. But, instead of overcoming evil with power, He conquered it with good.

The devil tempted Jesus to disobey God, to hate His enemies, to imitate the world's use of power. But, by His obedient self-sacrifice, Jesus won the decisive moral victory over evil. When Jesus died without sin, the devil had to concede defeat.

119

Applying the victory

Although the devil was decisively defeated at the cross, he still hasn't conceded total defeat. Although he was overthrown by the sinless blood of the Lamb, he hasn't been eliminated. He still opposes, tempts, deceives and attacks believers. I'm sure you've felt some of his blows, my friend!

If the devil had been eliminated at the cross, you wouldn't need to be an overcomer – because there'd be nobody to overcome. But if the devil hadn't been defeated at the cross, you couldn't be an overcomer, not even a tiny overcomer!

This paradox of *defeat without elimination* means God's Word:

⇒ *promises that you're seated and reigning with Christ, with all the forces of evil under His and your feet*

⇒ *but warns you not to stand against the enemy without the Lord's strength and armour*

⇒ *promises that Christ will keep you safe and that the evil one cannot touch you*

⇒ *but warns you to watch for the enemy who is prowling around seeking to devour you.*

Some believers emphasise the promises, while others focus on the warnings. God, however, wants you to live by *both* the promises *and* the warnings.

Celebrate the victory of the Lamb, dear friend. Live in the good of it at all time. Claim it in every difficult circumstance. Sprinkle the victorious blood over every lie and deception. But recognise too that the victory will not be complete until the last day.

For you, being an overcomer means:

⇒ *living with the sure knowledge that Satan still exists, but that his power has been fundamentally broken*

⇒ *recognising that your flesh still makes all manner of suggestions to you, but that these are essentially empty threats*

⇒ *realising that death still raises its ugly head, but that you've nothing to fear any more*

The blood has stripped the devil of his power; my friend, it's rendered him ineffective. Don't let him deceive you any more with false claims. Don't let him terrify you with empty threats.

Believe in the unlimited power of the blood, not in the broken power of the devil! Because of the blood, you can be certain of victory!

24

The blood deals with your failures

There's a little known story in the third chapter of Zechariah which describes a confrontation between Satan and one of God's servants.

The devil personally tempted Joshua, the Jewish high priest, to think that he was disqualified from God's service because of his 'dirty clothes'.

This attack came at a critical time in Jewish history. After forty years in exile, God's people had just begun to return to Jerusalem. Joshua's grandfather had been high priest when Jerusalem was captured, and had then been executed by Nebuchadnezzar. Joshua's father had been carried captive to Babylon, and it seems that Joshua was born in exile.

It must have been often suggested to Joshua that he didn't match up to his famous grandfather; and that he wasn't fit to be the high priest because he was a slave, born in exile, and so defiled (hence the dirty clothes). Satan seized upon this when he made his attack.

Satan's ploy

This is still one of the devil's commonest ploys, my friend. He whispers a temptation in one ear, then skips round the other side to accuse you in the other ear of having wrong thoughts!

I expect that he brings you constant reminders of past failures, long-forgiven sins, and a general sense of disqualification, defilement, inadequacy and unfitness for whatever God is calling you to do.

You must understand what the devil does. He attacks believers' consciences with the weapon of self-condemnation, and tries to trick them into a wrong sense of guilt at falling short of God's will.

Satan tempted Joshua to think that he was unfit for service because of his 'dirty clothes'. And he tempts you to think that God cannot and will not use you because you've failed God in the past and badly let Him down.

God's response

The book of Zechariah reports that the Lord Himself rebuked Satan, and that He then spoke to Joshua and the people around him.

Take away the filthy garments from him... See, I have removed your iniquity from you, and I will clothe you with rich robes. Zecharaiah 3:4

God says much the same to you, dear friend. He doesn't change the fact that you've fallen short of His will – that's history, you have failed, you have let Him down.

Instead, God delivers you from the consequences of failure. He delivers you from the paralysis of self-condemnation through the knowledge that the blood has delivered you from God's condemnation.

Christ was sacrificed once to take away the sins of many people; and He will appear a second time, not to bear sin, but to bring salvation to those waiting for Him. Hebrews 9:28 (NIV)

So, my friend, the next thing that the blood speaks to you is this: 'God has removed your sin – you're clean; you can serve Him; you can move on'.

All believers live in the tension between their awareness of their failures and their understanding of their justification.

Satan wants to deaden your sense of justification so that he can magnify your sense of failure, accuse you with constant reminders of past failings, and paralyse you with self-condemnation.

But God wants you to look at the blood, to listen to the blood, and to *sprinkle it over every one of your failures.*

Many believers have become utterly self-condemned by a failure or fault. They've spent far too long listening to these devilish lies:

⇒ *God can't use you because…*

⇒ *The reason nothing's happening is because…*

⇒ *Supposing everybody knew that…*

Don't let this happen to you, my friend. Listen to the blood. Sprinkle it over your failures. Do it now! Allow the blood to deal with your failures – and move on in confidence to serve God with all your heart and soul and strength.

25

The blood cries 'Glory'!

Many people are frightened of blood. Even a small drop makes them feel queasy, and they don't know what they'd do if they were faced with a wound pouring with blood. They can't understand how some people serve as doctors and nurses when they have to deal with so much blood!

Human blood may frighten you, my friend, but you must appreciate that Christ's blood is the most precious and wonderful substance in the world.

The cross, the place of God's own blood sacrifice, was the moment when His glory shone more brightly and clearly than at any time since the dawn of creation.

The blood shows, better than anything else in history, *what God is really like*. It decisively reveals His active presence in the world.

The great glory of the blood is that it's the supreme revelation of God's mercy, God's truth, God's grace, God's goodness, God's patience, God's peace, God's forgiveness, God's faith, God's righteousness, God's self-control, God's gentleness, God's self-effacement, God's justice, God's love, and so on, and so on!

Christ Jesus, whom God set forth to be a propitiation by His blood, through faith, to demonstrate His righteousness, because in His forbearance God had passed over the sins that were previously committed.　　　Romans 3:25

The blood speaks 'Glory!' to you, my friend, because it's the perfect revelation of God's holy nature. It shows you *exactly* what He is like.

Eternity won't be long enough for you to plumb the depths of God's nature. But, if you closely study the blood which was shed on the cross, you can get as clear a picture of God's nature as it's possible to get in this life.

It would take me several series of books to show you the full revelation of God in the blood! But let me point you briefly to one small aspect.

God's justice

Until the cross, God's justice had not been startlingly obvious on earth. Sinners sometimes prospered. Evil often went unpunished. And the Psalms ring with the puzzled cries of God's people at the injustice of life.

To many people in those days, God appeared to be unjust, or impotent, or morally indifferent. But God's long-suffering was a merciful postponement of judgement, not a final cancellation.

Eventually, at the cross through the blood, God fully revealed His perfect justice by condemning all sin in Christ.

On the cross through the blood, God gave visible proof of His justice by Himself bearing, in Christ, His just punishment of all the world's evil.

Since the blood on the cross, my friend, God can no longer be accused of condoning evil or of being unjust – because His justice in judging and punishing sin has, once-and-for-all, been clearly and convincingly shown.

This means that the blood now speaks these words to you: 'God is perfectly just'.

Satan will try to confuse you with the world's injustice and inequalities. He'll try to persuade you that the plight of the starving, the sick, the homeless, and so on, proves that God is unjust.

Don't listen to Satan. Listen to the blood instead. The blood proves that God utterly condemns the evil which causes poverty, sickness, sin and debt. It proves that God has completely punished – and Himself borne the punishment – this evil. The blood proves that God is just.

Once again, my dear friend, you may need to sprinkle the blood on your doubts. Let the blood speak its eternal truths to you!

Of course, God did not reveal only His justice at the cross. He revealed every aspect of His character, which is why the blood cries, 'Glory!'

From now on, whenever you doubt any part of God's nature, quickly turn to the cross and pour the blood over your doubts.

Its unlimited power, its total revelation of God's nature, will drive your doubts away. Hallelujah!

26

The blood promises life

The Old Testament book of Numbers contains a story about a time when God's people were very discouraged on their journey to the Promised Land.

Chapter twenty-one describes how the people complained about Moses and moaned about God's provision. In response, God sent some fiery serpents to lead them to repentance.

The sinful, snake-bitten Israelites were sure to die. However, in His grace, God provided them with a means of life.

The people could be saved from certain death only by looking to a bronze serpent which Moses had made and erected on a pole, according to the Lord's instructions.

If the people believed in God's provision, and showed this by looking at the pole, they lived. If they didn't look, they died from the snake poison.

God's gift of life

In the same way, my friend, Jesus came from heaven as God's gracious provision for all those who are certain to die.

He too was lifted on a pole, according to the Lord's instructions, as God's means of life for you.

When the blood flowed from His body, it was the greatest life-giving blood transfusion of eternity. Quite simply, dear friend. *His blood is your means of life!*

If you demonstrate your belief in God's gracious provision by looking to the One on the cross, you will receive God's new life. If, however, you don't look to the blood, you will certainly perish.

The blood is speaking to you, my friend, it's saying, 'Look and live!' The blood is promising you life – eternal life, abundant life, God's own life flowing through you! Hallelujah!

New life

Jesus' picture of a vine vividly expresses the idea of God's life flowing through His people.

Abide in me, and I in you. As the branch cannot bear fruit of itself, unless it abides in the vine, neither can you, unless you abide in Me. I am the vine, you are the branches. He who abides in Me, and I in him, bears much fruit; for without Me you can do nothing. John 15:4-5

This shows that the blood's life is meant to flow through you *continually*, and to keep on producing the character and quality of God's own life in you.

New life through the blood means both:

⇒ *a future spiritual existence in God's presence after your physical death*

⇒ *a present earthly existence which possesses all the characteristics of God's heavenly life*

Your blood-transfusion of new life is not merely a guaranteed first-class ticket to heaven (though it is!). It's also the gift of God's life to transform you into the likeness of God so that you increasingly reveal His family nature!

When you're reading the New Testament, you'll often come across the phrase 'new life'. This phrase sometimes points to your guaranteed future life in heaven; while at other times it points to your present life in Christ.

But no matter which of these it points to, every reference points to a new life which was brought into being by God at the cross through the blood.

Don't listen to your feelings my friend! And don't look in the mirror! All believers have times when they feel tired, discouraged, wrinkled and feeble.

Listen to the blood instead. Look at the cross and live! The blood promises you life. It promises God's life. It guarantees you a new quality of life on earth *and* an eternal existence in heaven.

It's up to you, my friend. What are you going to listen to? Where are you going to look? What are going to believe?

The precious blood pulsates with the life of Christ, and God wants to pump it through your veins at all times.

Open yourself to God's life. Don't waste any more time. Pause here for a while, and ask God to transform you by the blood.

27

The blood bids you 'Welcome!'

Do you remember what you learnt about the Day of Atonement? It was the one day in the Jewish year when the high priest could pass beyond the veil into the Holy of holies, into the tangible presence of God.

But the high priest could draw near to God only when sacrificial blood had dealt with his personal sin, and when the sacrifice of two goats had dealt with the sins of the whole people.

We can say that the blood 'spoke' to the high priest, and bade him enter into God's presence. Without the blood, the priest dare not pass through the veil. Because of the blood, he – and only he – could part the veil and enter into the Holy Place.

It was the same for Jesus, your Great High Priest, for it was only through His own shed blood that He entered – once-and-for-all – the Holy Place.

And it's exactly the same for you, my friend!

Therefore, brethren, having boldness to enter the Holy Place by the blood of Jesus, by a new and living way which He consecrated for us.

Hebrews 10:19

Because of His blood, you can now enter boldly into the tangible presence of God.

But have you?

Are you living in the presence of God? Or have you not fully exercised this blood-bought right?

At most football games, many supporters pass through the turnstiles an hour before the game begins, but don't take up their seats immediately. Instead, they spend time chatting and drinking under the stands, waiting until the last possible moment before climbing the steps to take their seats for the match.

In a similar way, there are many people who sincerely believe in God. They've trusted Christ for salvation. They're clutching their blood-bought 'ticket' into God's presence. But they haven't got round actually to entering into His presence and claiming God's covenant promises.

I hope you're not like this!

So what is the blood saying to you now, my friend? The book of Hebrews makes it plain:

Draw near with a true heart in full assurance of faith, having our hearts sprinkled from an evil conscience.   Hebrews 10:22

The blood is not saying, 'You can come in now'; rather, it's urging you 'Draw near'. It's bidding you, 'Welcome'. It's beseeching you to follow Christ through the veil into the Holy Place.

I know that it's hard to grasp some of these biblical pictures. But, dear friend, you must realise that this right to approach God's throne is one of the most glorious blessings of the blood.

And, unlike a ticket for a football match, you don't have to leave after ninety minutes! The blood is urging you into the Holy Place so that you can dwell there with God *for ever*!

Fellowship with God

I hope you've realised that this is just another way of describing your covenant relationship with God.

God wants you to enter into His presence because He wants to be with you and to bless you. It's amazing! The living God wants to spend as much time as possible with you, His dear friend.

Maybe you think that you're dull and boring. He's fascinated by you! Perhaps you think that you're not very special. He thinks you're wonderful! You might consider yourself to be rather unimportant. He loves you passionately and values you highly.

Christ has shed His blood especially so that *you* can draw near to God, can dwell in His intimate presence at all times, and can receive all His covenant blessings! Hallelujah!

The blessings of the presence

I trust, my friend, that you're starting to get to grips with the blood's unlimited power.

When you start to listen to the blood, and to respond to its urgent pleadings, you'll begin both to live in the immediate presence of God *and* to

137

enjoy the indescribable blessings which are associated with His covenant presence.

When you dwell in the presence of God, you'll be filled with a deep assurance of His love – you'll experience it and enjoy it!

You'll be able to make you needs and thoughts known to the Father in perfect freedom. You'll want for no good thing. You'll enjoy wholeness and healing. You'll be at rest and peace – because God Himself is with you.

You'll receive all the direction and instruction you need from God. You'll recognise the Spirit's quiet promptings. You'll discern the slightest hint of the Father's will – and will be pleased to obey it.

Once you enter more deeply into your covenant relationship with God, you'll soon discover that the holy presence of God is starting to have a wonderful effect on you.

God's presence will 'rub off' onto you, and will fill you with His humility, His patience, His joy and His love. When you dwell with God, my dear friend, the Holy One will make you holy.

And that, I hope, is now your dearest wish.

Your faith declaration

"I declare and confess that God is speaking to me through the shed blood of Christ. I am listening to the blood and I am looking to the blood at all times. I am allowing the blood to remind me of all that God has done for me through the cross.

The blood proves that God loves me, and I sprinkle the blood on every testing circumstance, every challenging situation, every difficulty and setback. I cover them with the proof of God's love.

The blood assures me that I have been changed into an overcomer, and I sprinkle the blood on every lie and deception of the enemy. I affirm that the devil exists, but that his power has been broken. I believe in the unlimited power of the blood, and not in the broken power of the devil.

The blood reminds me that God has dealt with my failures and has delivered me from God's condemnation. I will not condemn myself again. I sprinkle the blood on all my failures, and will not listen to the devil's lies any more.

I affirm that I can serve God, that I have been called to serve God, and that I will serve God. By the blood's unlimited power, I am now useful to Him. Praise His holy name."

28

The cross is central

You've now reached the last section of this book about the unlimited power of the blood.

You've seen that a crimson thread runs through the Bible from Eden to Calvary.

You've noticed how the shadow of the cross falls on the whole Bible, and how the Old Testament sacrifices and covenants point forward to the cross.

You've begun to appreciate what God has done for you on the cross through the blood. Nothing should ever be the same again for you!

You've learnt that God wants to keep using the blood to bring practical changes to your life – to handle adversity better and to make your thoughts and behaviour more like His.

And you've started to listen to the blood, to sprinkle it over your doubts and fears, to enter more deeply into the holy presence of God.

But what now, dear friend?

Where do you go from here?

Is God calling you into His holy presence just to enjoy His blessings of salvation, provision and healing? Or might He be calling you to serve Him in some new way?

Obviously, I don't know what God has in store for you. I don't know what He will ask you to do or where He will send you to go. But I do know that your service, indeed your whole life, should be characterised by the blood and the cross.

At the start of this book, I pointed out that there can be few people in the world who do not recognise that a simple wooden cross is the universal symbol of our Christian faith.

Quite simply, the cross means Christ, and Christ means the cross. If you're going to be a Christian – to be a 'Christ person' – you must also be a 'cross person'. You cannot follow Christ, my friend, and sideline the cross – it's just not possible.

Jesus and the cross

The Bible makes it plain that the cross is the heart of God's purposes for Jesus, and that the cross is at the heart of who Jesus is.

My soul is troubled and what shall I say? Father save Me from this hour? But for this purpose I came to this hour. Father, glorify Your name.

John 12:27

Jesus spoke these words when He was preparing for the cross. They show that the pressure of the cross had started to touch the core of His life.

In His humanity, Jesus wanted to ask God to save Him from the cross. But He knew that He'd come for the purpose of the cross, so – after a great struggle – He asked the Father to glorify His name.

Can you see, my friend? *The cross is the key to bringing glory to God.* When the cross is central to your life and your service, you'll glorify God in everything that you do and in all that you are!

Some believers realise that the cross is important, but they don't appreciate just how important! It's central to *everything*! It's the foundation and fulfilment of faith! The cross was God's purpose for Jesus, and the cross is His purpose for you!

142

Do you want to see God's purposes fulfilled in-and-for your life? Of course you do! So come to the cross, dear friend. Cling to the cross! Carry the cross! Live according to the cross – and God will be greatly glorified through you.

The empty cross

Some churches contain a cross which still bears the broken body of Jesus. Although this may help them to appreciate Christ's sufferings, it proclaims an inaccurate message about the cross.

Christ's body is not on the cross any more! The cross is empty! The tomb is empty! Jesus is alive! He was raised from the dead and is seated at the right hand of the Father to apply all the achievements of the cross in your life.

As you read this, my dear friend, Jesus is praying for you in heaven. He's interceding with the Father about you. He's taking the cross and is applying it to your life on the basis of the blood.

You need the cross and the blood, for they give you access into *everything* that God has for you. Will you come the way of the cross? Will you live the way of the cross? When you allow the cross to dominate everything, you'll be on the way to glory!

29

The cross is a mystery

From the moment in Eden when God announced that the Seed would bruise the Serpent's head, history began to wind towards the cross.

All the Old Testament stories lead towards the coming of the Messiah, and all the Gospels lead towards the cross. As you read the Scriptures, it's as though you're ascending a mountain range of revelation, and the highest peak of all is Calvary.

When you struggle to the top (to the climax of the Bible, the climax of history) you don't find golden gates, rejoicing angels and the throne of God; instead there's a rough wooden cross, some rusty Roman nails, and a dead and bloodied Saviour.

This has to be a mystery of God, for no human mind would ever conceive such a climax.

⇒ *The Messiah, the Conqueror, the Deliverer, the King, hangs limp and dead in the sun.*

⇒ *The greatest moral teacher is abandoned by the perfect God.*

⇒ *The sinless, loving, forgiving Only Son is whipped by men and punished by His Father.*

Truly the cross is a great mystery!

The mystery of God

Throughout this book, I've tried to unravel something of the mystery of the cross and the blood. But it is a mystery. Don't forget that.

It seems that God brought together all the mysteries of the Universe, piled them into one cross-shaped revelation, and announced – 'This is my mystery! This is my revelation!'

It's as though, in the cross, God is demonstrating that He's bigger and greater and wiser than the full wisdom of all humanity.

The cross should boggle your mind, dear friend. All you can do is kneel at its foot and worship the One who bled and died and rose again.

The mystery for the nations

Do you want to startle society? Do you want to shock the people around you into putting down their silly ideas? Do you want to say something which will change the world forever?

You can. You can speak about the cross.

Kings shall shut their mouths at Him; for what had not been told them they shall see, and what they had not heard they shall consider. Who has believed our report? Isaiah 52:15 – 53:1

The rulers of this world can't speak in the presence of the crucified Saviour. The mystery of the cross is beyond human belief, and – without the Spirit's help, my friend – you won't believe it too.

The cross is not a private matter. It's a *public* revelation of God, and you're called to take the cross – to live and proclaim it publicly in your area.

Hundreds watched when Jesus was slain. Many made little sense of the mystery. But some did.

When the centurion and those with him who were guarding Jesus saw the earthquake and the things that had happened, they feared greatly, saying, 'Truly this was the Son of God'. Matthew 27:54

In the same way, your cross-life and cross-words will puzzle many people; but some modern-day Centurions and soldiers will recognise that the Son of God is at the centre of your life, and they will bow their knees to Him.

The ugly cross

Some of you may have fingered your shiny gold crosses with pride in the last chapter, when I said that crosses bearing Christ's body were unhelpful.

I'm sorry, my friend, but the beautiful gold objects that some believers wear round their necks are equally unhelpful!

The cross isn't nice; it's ugly and terrible. It commemorates the worst thing that's happened. It celebrates the most pain that's ever been inflicted and endured. It records the worst crime in history.

And God let it happen. In fact, He planned every small detail! That's the mystery!

Human freedom

At one level, the cross occurred because God gave us the freedom to slap Him in the face. He's given us the freedom to ignore Him, to oppose Him, even to hammer nails into Him.

At this level, the cross demonstrates to the nations the full consequences of lives turned against God. It reveals how people live until they turn to Jesus.

Yet, at another level, the cross occurred because God planned it. He prophesied it. He prepared it. He worked out the details. He was in full control.

Now this really is some mystery! How can God be totally sovereign and humanity be totally free – both at the same time? If you've the answer, my friend, I'd really like to hear it!

Nevertheless, side by side in the cross, we find the best and the worst – sin and perfection, forgiveness and condemnation, God and humanity, love and justice, hope and disappointment, death and resurrection. And in this mystery is *your* salvation, and the salvation of the whole world.

No matter the clashes and conflicts in your life, my friend. No matter the pain and suffering, the hurt caused by human freedom, the cross announces to you that God is in full control.

He is working out your salvation. He is bringing you forgiveness, hope, healing and resurrection. Your circumstances may be a puzzling mystery, but the cross implores you to trust the One in control.

30

The cross is the key

We've talked a lot about your blood-covenant relationship with God in this book. This is so important that I want to underline it one last time!

Never forget, dear friend, that the blood on the cross is the key to your relationship with God.

When you look at the cross and listen to the blood, you see the selfless sacrifice of Christ for guilty sinners – so *that* God can accept those sinners, forgive them of their sin, redeem them for Himself, declare them righteous, and reconcile them with Himself.

Hallelujah! What a Saviour!

For whom is the cross?

Let me ask you an important question. For whom did Jesus die on the cross? For whom did He shed His blood on the cross? Think about it for a moment. The answer is the key to your relationship with God and your attitude to other people.

Did Jesus die for pure, nice, theologically sound people – like you and me?

Of course not. He died for *guilty sinners* because He loves each one of them with infinite passion.

God demonstrates His own love towards us, in that while we were still sinners, Christ died for us.

Romans 5:8

When some people have been believers for a while, they start to think that they're in a relationship with God because they're good. They don't swear. They don't gamble. They read their Bibles and pray. They support overseas missions.

They think that they're God's friends because they're good – and they make sure that their human friends are men and women who are equally good!

This gives people the impression that church is for saints and the cross is for saints. God forgive us!

Let me tell you, my friend, that the only people who can enjoy a covenant relationship with God are *guilty sinners*. If you're not a guilty sinner, you haven't a hope of salvation!

The law court

The apostle Paul often uses the language of the law courts. If we use Paul's picture, you're the prisoner in the dock, Satan is the prosecution council, God is the Judge, and Jesus is the defence council.

The devil doesn't need to lie to prove that you're a sinner, for you know that the charges are true. God opens His mouth to sentence you, when your Advocate stands to speak.

'Let me tell you something about this sinner,' He says. 'I died for him on the cross. My blood pleads for him. My blood covers him.'

The Judge smiles at you, announces, 'Not guilty', and Satan explodes. 'Not guilty!' he screams, 'What about his sin?'

Your Advocate leans forward and quietly says, 'They're under the blood; they're under the blood'.

Make no mistake, dear friend. You know what you've thought and done. If you did not have an

Advocate, and if He'd not been to the cross, God would have to condemn you to eternal punishment.

But you do have an Advocate. He has been to the cross. The blood does plead for you – and so God declares you His friend, adopts you as His child, and welcomes you into His presence.

Do you get the message, my friend?

⇒ *Forgiveness is for the guilty*

⇒ *Salvation is for sinners*

⇒ *Redemption is for slaves*

⇒ *Justification is for the unrighteous*

⇒ *Reconciliation is for God's enemies*

⇒ *Cleansing is for the filthy*

⇒ *Release is for Satan's captives*

⇒ *Sanctification is for the unsanctified*

Jesus came not to call the righteous, but sinners to repentance. He called you to Himself because you were a filthy, guilty, rebellious sinner – there was no other reason.

Because your salvation (your covenant relationship with God) is 'none of you and all of Him', you know for certain that you're saved today, that you'll be saved tomorrow, and that you'll be saved when Jesus returns in glory.

Nothing will ever separate you from the love of God in Christ Jesus!

But do you know why this? Is it:

⇒ *Because of your goodness or because of the cross?*

⇒ *Because of your doctrine or because of the blood?*

I hope that you know the right answer by now!

Never forget, dear friend, that the cross of Jesus Christ is the only key to your unbreakable covenant relationship with God.

31

Carry the cross

When Jesus' disciples finally realised that He was the Messiah, He explained to them what this meant.

Jesus began to show His disciples that He must go to Jerusalem, and suffer many things... and be killed, and be raised again the third day.

Matthew 16:21

The disciples protested at this news. They didn't believe that God's way for the Messiah could involve suffering, rejection, death and resurrection.

Jesus rebuked them, and said that God's demand for the cross applied *to them* as well as to Him.

If anyone desires to come after Me, let him deny himself, and take up his cross daily, and follow Me.   Luke 9:23

These words were spoken to disciples who were already following Jesus, who'd listened to His teaching and seen Him work signs and wonders.

Now that they knew the truth about where Jesus was going, He set them free to choose either the cross or their own path.

You're in a similar position to those disciples, dear friend. You're a believer. You listen to Jesus. Perhaps you've seen Him work a wonder or two. And now that you know the truth about the cross, He's asking you to carry the cross – *every day*.

Cling to the cross

Of course, you can't carry the cross without clinging to the cross. And if you've tasted what it means to be justified by faith, to have you're sins forgiven by the blood, you'll surely want to go on clinging to the cross!

You don't have to earn God's favour, my friend, for it's freely given. And you can never be more acceptable to God than you are *right now*.

Although the devil will keep on accusing you of being a sinner until the day you die, the things that he says to you won't be true!

⇒ *He'll call you a sinner, but you can tell him that you're clothed in God's righteousness.*

⇒ *He'll try to make you think that you've got to do something to please God.*

⇒ *He'll call you a fraud, but you can tell him that you're a sanctified child of God.*

Ignore his rubbish! Don't listen to his lies! You can't earn God's favour; you can only cling to the cross. Don't let go for a moment!

Carry the cross

However, Jesus didn't tell His disciples to stand still and cling to the cross; He told them to follow Him and carry the cross.

You can't carry the cross, my friend, without clinging to it, but you can cling to the cross and not carry it! I think God's telling you to get moving!

He's calling you to depend completely on the cross, but He's also commissioning you to carry the cross into the world. He doesn't want you to hide in a religious cross-clingers' club, He wants you to follow Jesus and carry the cross out into the world.

What does it mean?

Carrying the cross means allowing the cross to shape your attitudes and actions. It means giving not getting, sacrificial service not selfish self-seeking, being unconcerned about yourself and concerned only about Christ.

Carrying the cross means having your eyes so fixed on the One you're following that you're blind to the path which is too steep for you, and deaf to the pain which pleads with you to stop.

It means knowing that nothing in this life can compare to the glory which is waiting for you – if you stick close to His bent and beaten back.

Your call to carry the cross is not a calamity, my friend; it's the fruit of your commitment. It's not a sad accident; it's your spiritual appointment; and it's not the end of everything – rather, it's the beginning of your abundant life with Christ!

Proclaim the cross

If you think back to the last chapter, you'll remember I said that the cross is the key to your attitude to other people as well as the key to your relationship with God.

Because Jesus died on the cross for guilty sinners, believers who carry the cross have a special responsibility to proclaim the cross to sinners.

Carrying the cross doesn't mean literally lugging a huge wooden gibbet around with you! It's means depending on the blood, living the sacrificial cross life, and proclaiming and demonstrating the message of the cross to those for whom Jesus died.

You've got to start talking about the cross, my friend. You mustn't keep such wonderful truths to yourself any more. You mustn't remain silent when people are living and dying without hope.

Don't argue with people, just talk about the cross in a way that they understand. Never be ashamed of the cross, for it's the best news in the world.

The cross really is the message for today; and if we had a generation of people who lived and proclaimed the cross, our nations would be saved.

And I, if I am lifted up from the earth, will draw all peoples to Myself. John 12:32

Carry the cross, my friend; preach it and live it wherever you are. Talk about the cross of Jesus at all times – for it's the message that God uses to draw people to Himself.

Follow Jesus

I'm certain that Jesus is calling you, my dear friend, to carry the cross; but He's not sending you out on your own. He's calling you to follow Him and carry the cross, to join Him in the fellowship of the cross, to receive His anointing of the cross.

Think about Jesus for a few moments.

He did not shout or raise His voice. He was gentle with the weak, but utterly just. He gave sight to the blind and liberated prisoners, yet He exhausted Himself and appeared – at times – to work in vain.

He was despised and rejected, familiar with suffering. He was punished, struck, pierced, wounded and burdened by God.

He was courageous, patient, pure and meek. His only reward was with God, and God was His only source of strength and speech.

Although His back was beaten, His beard plucked, and His face spat upon, He set His face like flint and persevered with His arduous task.

And this is the wonderful One who is now calling you to follow Him down the road to glory. Follow Him, my friend, please follow Him with the cross – wherever in the world He may lead you.

Other books in this LIVING WORD SERIES include:

- Prayer that gets answers
- God's Word in my mouth
- Household Salvation

For a full catalogue of Colin Dye ministry products, please contact:

Dovewell Mail Order
PO Box 9161
London
W3 6GS
England

Tel: 0171 727 8684
Fax: 0171 727 8716
e mail: ken-temp@dircon.co.uk
web site: http/www.ken-temp.org.uk